First Steps in SAP® FI Configuration

Ann Cacciottoli

Thank you for purchasing this book from Espresso Tutorials!

Like a cup of espresso coffee, Espresso Tutorials SAP books are concise and effective. We know that your time is valuable and we deliver information in a succinct and straightforward manner. It only takes our readers a short amount of time to consume SAP concepts. Our books are well recognized in the industry for leveraging tutorial-style instruction and videos to show you step by step how to successfully work with SAP.

Check out our YouTube channel to watch our videos at
https://www.youtube.com/user/EspressoTutorials.

If you are interested in SAP Finance and Controlling, join us at
http://www.fico-forum.com/forum2/
to get your SAP questions answered and contribute to discussions.

Related titles from Espresso Tutorials:

▶ Dieter Schlagenhauf & Jörg Siebert: SAP® Fixed Assets Accounting (FI AA)
   http://5023.espresso-tutorials.com

▶ Thomas Michael: Reporting for SAP® Asset Accounting
   http://5029.espresso-tutorials.com

▶ Lennart B. Ullmann & Claus Wild: Electronic Bank Statement and Lockbox in SAP® ERP
   http://5056.espresso-tutorials.com

▶ Stephen Birchall: Invoice Verification for SAP®
   http://5073.espresso-tutorials.com

▶ Janet Salmon & Ulrich Schlüter: SAP® HANA for ERP Financials, 2nd edition
   http://5092.espresso-tutorials.com

▶ Ann Cacciottolli: First Steps in SAP® Financial Accounting (FI)
   http://5095.espresso-tutorials.com

Ann Cacciottoli
First Steps in SAP® FI Configuration

ISBN:	978-1-52385510-0
Editor:	Lisa Jackson
Cover Design:	Philip Esch, Martin Munzel
Cover Photo:	fotolia #67003741 © MIGUEL GARCIA SAAVED
Interior Design:	Johann-Christian Hanke

All rights reserved.

1st Edition 2016, Gleichen

© 2016 by Espresso Tutorials GmbH

URL: *www.espresso-tutorials.com*

Feedback
We greatly appreciate any kind of feedback you have concerning this book. Please mail us at *info@espresso-tutorials.com*.

Table of Contents

Preface

Recently, I undertook the challenge of writing a book intended to help individuals new to SAP software, or new to an accounting environment, develop some basic knowledge and skills in SAP FI (financial accounting).

While putting together illustrations for the book, I needed to perform many configuration steps in order to create examples and screen captures in the international data exchange service (IDES) environment. The book, *First Steps in SAP Financial Accounting (FI)* includes an appendix with directions for completing the basic configuration to enable the reader to use an IDES environment for configuration. However, the brief instructions lack substantive explanations.

This book, *First Steps in Configuring SAP FI,* can be used as a companion text to *First Steps in SAP Financial Accounting (FI)* as it provides explanations and logic behind the configuration required for the exercises in *First Steps in SAP Financial Accounting (FI)*.

This book is meant to be a stand-alone text, presenting the basic configuration necessary for a basic SAP environment where general ledger, accounts receivable, and accounts payable transactions can be entered.

How this book is organized

Chapter 1 provides instruction on creating a company code. This configuration is necessary for the entire SAP FI module. The remaining chapters demonstrate the configuration needed for working with the individual modules. Chapter 2 focuses on general ledger (GL), Chapter 3 on accounts receivable (AR), and Chapter 4 on accounts payable (AP).

The chapters provide a step-by-step guide for configuration and can also serve as a future reference. The beginner to SAP software should be able to quickly develop the minimal skills needed to navigate in the SAP FI application and become proficient in configuring the SAP FI modules.

Accessing configuration transactions

Configuration transactions are not part of the SAP EASY ACCESS menu. Rather, as shown throughout the book, you must access the transaction from the *SAP Implementation Guide* (SAP IMG) menu path.

Transport requests

You will be prompted to create a *transport request.* A transport request is a means to collect the information being entered so it may be "transported" to another SAP environment. The transport functionality enables configuration to take place in a development environment and transported to a productive environment. The discussion of transporting a configuration between various environments is beyond the scope of this text; however, you will be able to create a transport in order to complete a configuration.

We have added a few icons to highlight important information. These include:

Tips

 Tips highlight information concerning more details about the subject being described and/or additional background information.

Attention

 Attention notices draw attention to information that you should be aware of when you go through the examples from this book on your own.

Finally, a note concerning the copyright: All screenshots printed in this book are the copyright of SAP SE. All rights are reserved by SAP SE. Copyright pertains to all SAP images in this publication. For simplification, we will not mention this specifically underneath every screenshot.

1 First steps in configuring a general ledger

This chapter introduces the most common object in SAP, a company code. Company codes are defined and followed by the steps to configure a company code and create a chart of accounts in order that general ledger transactions may be processed.

The general ledger contains a record of financial business transactions. It is the primary source of information for preparing a company's financial statements. In SAP FI, general ledger transactions are recorded in general ledger accounts which are assigned to one or more company codes.

1.1 What is a company code?

To start, consider the basic premise of double-entry bookkeeping, the *accounting formula:*

$$Assets - Liabilities = Owner's\ Equity$$

At the end of any accounting period, the net of all entries in revenue and expense accounts is an increase (or decrease if expenses are greater than revenue) in owner's equity. The summation of the net increase or decrease in all of the revenue and expense accounts provides a picture of the results of the business activity. The results of business activity are presented in a somewhat standard format known as a *profit & loss* or *P&L* report. The summation of all assets minus liabilities provides a picture of the net worth of the business. The net worth of a business is presented in a report known as a *balance sheet.*

A company code generally represents a legal entity. It is the lowest level at which true balance sheet and profit & loss statements can be created. The accounting formula holds true when summing all transactions for any one company code.

1.2 Create a company code

There are several steps involved in creating a company code before it can be used for posting transactions:

▶ Name the company code

▶ Define the company code global parameters

▶ Assign the company code to controlling area

Create company code

First, enter the SAP REFERENCE IMG (SPRO) menu by following the steps below:

1. Type SPRO in the command field (as shown in Figure 1.1) and then press ⌈Enter⌋.

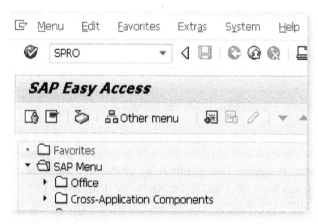

Figure 1.1: Create company code, step 1

2. Click on SAP REFERENCE IMG as shown in Figure 1.2.

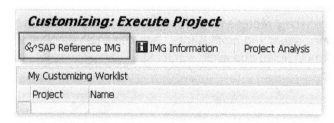

Figure 1.2: Create company code, step 2

3. From the SAP CUSTOMIZING IMPLEMENTATION GUIDE menu, navigate to ENTERPRISE STRUCTURE • DEFINITION • FINANCIAL ACCOUNTING • EDIT, COPY, DELETE, CHECK COMPANY CODE as shown in Figure 1.3.

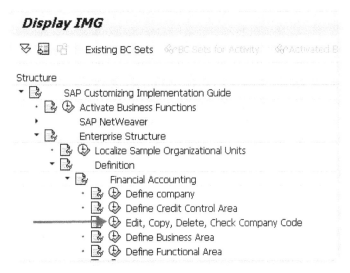

Figure 1.3: Create company code, steps 3 and 4

4. Click ⊕ to execute the transaction.

5. Double click on EDIT COMPANY CODE DATA as shown in Figure 1.4.

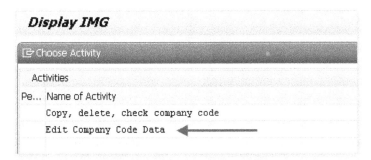

Figure 1.4: Create company code, step 5

A list of existing company codes is presented. You have the choice of creating an entirely new entry or cloning an existing company code to a new record. SAP FI is delivered with sample company codes and the easiest way to create a new company code is to clone one of the samples.

Transaction code for company code creation

 Rather than navigate to the SAP IMG menu, you can type transaction code OX02 in the command field and press [Enter] to get directly to step 6 below.

---

6. From the list of company codes presented (Figure 1.5), scroll to the company code that you want to clone. Select the company code by clicking on the box to the left of the company code. Then click the COPY AS icon.

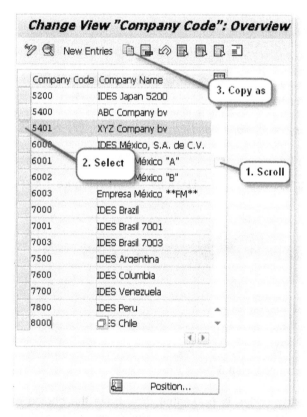

Figure 1.5: Create company code, step 6

7. Change the applicable information for the company code as desired (Figure 1.6) and then press [Enter].

8. Enter address information as shown in Figure 1.7.

12

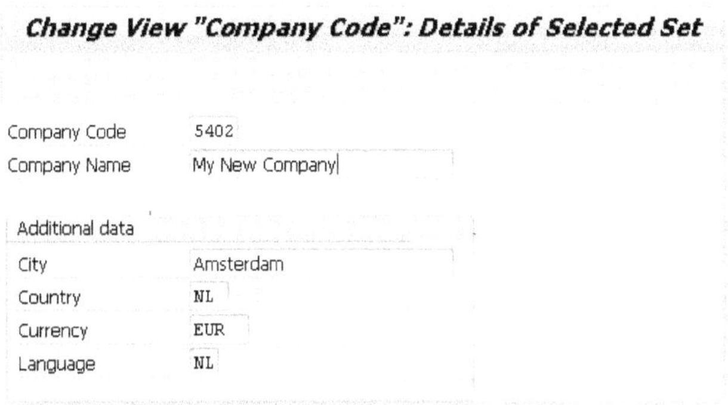

Change View "Company Code": Details of Selected Set

| Company Code | 5402 |
| Company Name | My New Company |

Additional data

City	Amsterdam
Country	NL
Currency	EUR
Language	NL

Figure 1.6: Create company code, step 7

Edit address: 5402

Name

| Title | Mr. |
| Name | Joergberg |

Search Terms

| Search term 1/2 | IDES |

Street Address

Street/House number	Surinamestratt 27
Postal Code/City	2585 GJ Den Haag
Country	NL Netherlands Region
Time zone	CET

PO Box Address

PO Box	90922
Postal Code	2585 GJ
Company postal code	

Communication

Language	Dutch	Other Communication...
Telephone		Extension
Mobile Phone	
Fax		Extension
E-Mail	
Standard Comm.Method	
Data line	
Telebox	

| Comments | |

✔ ✗ 🖶 Preview International Versions ✖

Figure 1.7: Create company code, step 8

9. Use dropdown menus (Figure 1.8) to make selections.

Figure 1.8: Create company code, step 9

10. Choose an option at the bottom of the screen (Figure 1.9) to enter additional address fields, preview a formatted address for printing, check the address, save the information, or cancel changes. Then click the SAVE icon 🖫 to save the new company code.

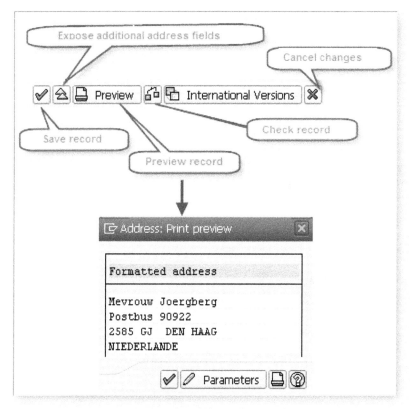

Figure 1.9: Create company code, step 10

11. If presented with the PROMPT FOR CUSTOMIZING REQUEST dialog box, click the CREATE icon ⬜ (Figure 1.10).

Figure 1.10: Create company code, step 11

12. Enter a description for the transport request as shown in Figure 1.11 and click the SAVE icon 💾.

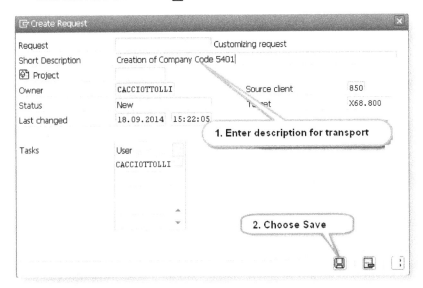

Figure 1.11: Create company code, step 12

13. Click the ENTER CONTINUE icon ✅ to save the transport request (Figure 1.12).

Figure 1.12: Create company code, step 13

15

14. Note the information message at the bottom of the screen: "Data was saved" (Figure 1.13). Click the BACK icon  at the upper left corner of the screen to return to the SAP EASY ACCESS menu.

Figure 1.13: Create company code, step 14

To enter a new company code without cloning, follow the steps above through step 5 then ...

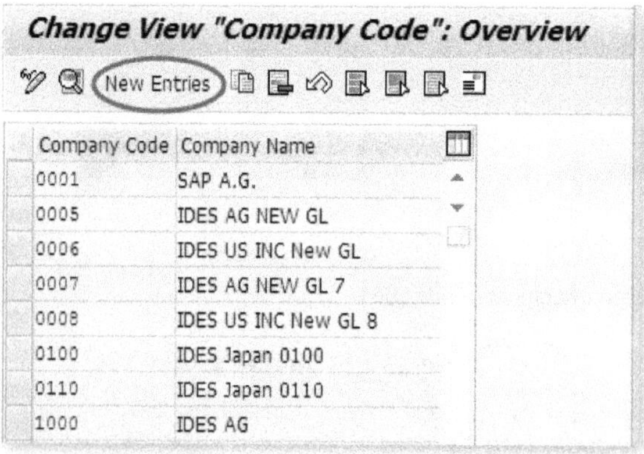

Figure 1.14: Create company code, alternate step 6

6. ... select New Entries (Figure 1.14). Enter information about the company code and then click ≡ to enter detailed address information.

7. Repeat steps 7 through 14 above as applicable.

Define company code global parameters

What are global parameters?

Global parameters provide information about company codes, some of which is required before postings can be made. For example, the SAP FI system must reference a chart of accounts (covered in Section 1.3) in order to find the general ledger accounts valid for the company code. There are many global parameters that can be set for company codes. The table below lists required or most common codes. A thorough presentation of the SAP functionality controlled by many of the parameters is beyond the scope of this text; however, each parameter is included in the table below. Parameters marked * are required before postings can be made.

Parameter	Description
CHART OF ACCTS*	A chart of accounts is a listing of the *accounts* that may be used for posting.
COUNTRY CHART/ACCTS	Some countries have a statutory chart of accounts. If this alternate chart of accounts is required, the chart of accounts name should be entered in this parameter.
COMPANY	COMPANY is an organization level higher than company code; it is used with SAP's legal consolidations module (ECCS). COMPANY can contain more than one company code, but a company code can only be assigned to one company.
FM AREA	Financial management (FM) areas are used with the SAP Treasury module.

17

Parameter	Description
CREDIT CONTROL AREA*	This parameter is used to control credit limits for customers. A credit limit can be assigned to many company codes, but a company code can only be assigned to one credit limit.
FISCAL YEAR VARIANT*	A fiscal year variant is a definition of the posting periods contained in a fiscal year as well the beginning month for the fiscal year. It is common for companies to have 12 posting periods (representing the months in a year), 4 adjustment periods, and a year beginning in January to coincide with the calendar year. However, some companies might have a fiscal year that begins on October 1 and ends September 30. Still, others might have 52 weekly periods. You can configure fiscal year variants to accommodate various scenarios. For the examples in this book, the standard fiscal year variant "K4" represents the calendar months plus 4 adjusting periods.
EXT.CO.CODE	If the SAP application will communicate with external systems, this indicator should be set.
GLOBAL COCODE	If the EXT.CO.CODE indicator has been selected, then the external company code must be entered in this parameter.
COMPANY IS PRODUCTIVE	When this indicator is set, it will not be possible to delete transactions. (In a test system, it is often useful to delete all of the transactions for a company code). This indicator should be set in the production environment.
VAT REGISTRATION NO.	This parameter is used to record the Value Added Tax registration number used by companies in the European Union (EU) in order that tax filings may include the number.

Parameter	Description
DOCUMENT ENTRY SCREEN VARIANT	There are some countries where specific data is needed when entering accounting documents. Fields for this data can be included on entry screens with the use of screen variants which can be assigned to a company code. The creation of screen variants is beyond the scope of this text.
BUSINESS AREA FIN. STATE-MENTS	This is one more organizational unit available in SAP FI. It can be used to aggregate data by product group or market. If this indicator is selected, the business area field will be required when posting documents. Financial statements can be created by business area.
FIELD STATUS VARIANT*	In SAP FI, field status groups are defined to indicate which fields are mandatory, optional, or suppressed when entering documents. The FIELD STATUS VARIANT is a collection of field status groups. SAP FI comes with delivered field status groups. The creation and/or change of field status groups are beyond the scope of this text.
PROPOSE FISCAL YEAR	When this indicator is selected, the fiscal year will be part of the primary key field that is used for looking up documents. SAP FI recommends that this indicator be selected to reduce the time required for searching document.
PSTNG PERIOD VARIANT*	A posting period variant controls which fiscal periods are open for transaction processing. After a period is closed, for example, you can lock it down so that no additional entries are made in that period. Because different company codes may have different require-ments, the lock down is done by using a posting peri-od variant. Different company codes can be assigned different posting period variants.
DEFINE DEFAULT VALUE DATE	When this indicator is selected, the current (system) date will default when documents are created.

Parameter	Description
MAX. EXCHANGE RATE DEVIATION	When transactions in a currency other than the company code currency are entered in SAP FI, both the company code currency and transaction currency are included in the transaction. An exchange rate taken from exchange rate tables can be applied to the transaction, or you can enter both amounts. By entering a percentage value in this parameter, you can cause the system to issue warning messages whenever a transaction is entered where the difference between the transaction currency and the company code currency vary from exchange rate tables. Exchange rate tables contain historical exchange rates between currencies and are generally updated on a periodic (including daily) basis, depending on business requirements.
NO FOREX RATE DIFF. WHEN CLEARING LC	Exchange rate differences occur, for example, when a customer receivable is recorded at one exchange rate and paid when the exchange rate has changed. If this indicator is selected, when documents are cleared, the amount stored as company code currency will be used for clearing. This indicator also controls how postings are done to account for the gains/losses due to the exchange rate differences.
SAMPLE ACCT RULES VAR.	SAP FI provides for the creation of sample accounts with specific rules that can then be applied when accounts are copied from one company code to another. Different rule variants can be created for each company code.
TAX BASE IS NET VALUE	If this indicator is selected, the basis for sales tax calculations will be after a discount has been applied.
WORKFLOW VARIANT	Workflow enables specific routing of documents for approval after entry and before posting. Workflow variants allow routings for different company codes to be grouped; several company codes can share the same variant.
DISCOUNT BASE IS NET VALUE	If this indicator is selected, sales and use taxes are not included in the calculation of cash discounts.

Parameter	Description
INFLATION METHOD	SAP FI has a solution for inflation accounting, and if used, an inflation method must be assigned to the company code.
FINANCIAL ASSETS MGMT ACTIVE	This indicator is set when using the SAP Asset Accounting module.
CRCY TRANSL. FOR TAX	This parameter allows for different exchange rates to be applied to tax amounts other than amounts already on the document.
PURCHASE ACCT PROC.	This indicator is set when purchase account processing is used. Postings of material transactions involve specific details, for example, the freight may not be included in the material account.
COCD->CO AREA*	A setting of "1" is used when there will be only one company code in the controlling area. A setting of "2" is used when there will be more than one company code in the controlling area and cross-company accounting is active.
JV ACCOUNTING ACTIVE	This indicator is set if joint venture (JV) accounting is a business requirement for the company code (common in oil and gas companies).
COST OF SALES ACCOUNTING ACTV.	Cost of sales accounting is a method of accounting where the cost of goods sold is reported in the income statement when the revenues are reported. The cost of goods produced and not sold is part of the balance sheet. The use of cost of sales accounting enables the use of the field functional area for reporting purposes and can be derived from other data on the transaction (cost center, cost element, or general ledger account).
HEDGE REQUEST ACTIVE	This indicator is used along with advanced functionality that is part of the SAP Treasury module.
NEGATIVE POSTINGS PERMITTED	If this indicator is set, then original and reversing entries will not display. The account balance will be adjusted as both documents were never posted. You will need to configure settings for document types and reversal reasons in order to use this functionality.

Parameter	Description
ENABLE AMOUNT SPLIT	This indicator enables an invoice or credit memo to be split across accounts.
ACTIVATE CM	This indicator is selected if cash management functions from the SAP Treasury module will be used for the company code.
TAX REPORTING DATE ACTIVE	Business requirements may call for a tax reporting date on a document to be different than the document date. This indicator, along with other configuration data, will enable a tax reporting date.
MANAGE POSTG PERIOD	This indicator, applicable for parallel ledgers, is used along with configuration for non-leading ledgers. It is used when the posting period and fiscal year variants for the leading ledger and non-leading ledgers will not be the same.

Table 1.1: Company code global parameters

Assign global parameters to a company code

Just as with defining company codes, the assignment of a global parameter transaction is not part of the SAP EASY ACCESS menu and you must enter the SAP REFERENCE IMG menu by following the steps below:

1. Type SPRO in the command field and then press ⌞Enter⌟ (Figure 1.15).

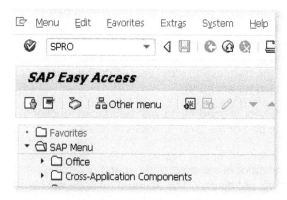

Figure 1.15: Assign global parameters to a company code, step 1

2. Click on SAP REFERENCE IMG (Figure 1.16).

Figure 1.16: Assign global parameters to a company code, step 2

3. From the SAP CUSTOMIZING IMPLEMENTATION GUIDE menu navigate to FINANCIAL ACCOUNTING (NEW) • FINANCIAL ACCOUNTING GLOBAL SETTINGS (NEW) • GLOBAL PARAMETERS FOR COMPANY CODE • ENTER GLOBAL PARAMETERS (Figure 1.17).

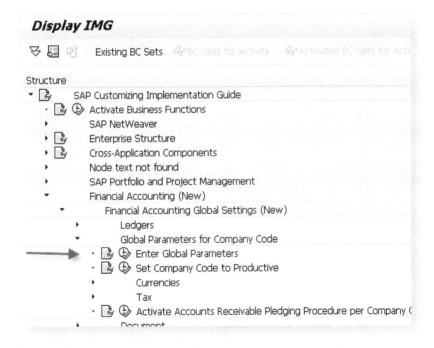

Figure 1.17: Assign global parameters to company code, step 3

Transaction for assigning global parameters

 Rather than navigate to the SAP REFERENCE IMG menu, you can type transaction code OBY6 in the command field and press [Enter] to get directly to step 4 below.

4. Scroll to the company code you are assigning global parameters to and click on the DETAILS icon 🔍 or press [F2] (Figure 1.18).

5. Make entries for desired fields as shown in Figure 1.19.

6. Save changes by clicking the SAVE icon 💾. Note the message returned that the "Data was saved" (Figure 1.20).

Display View "Company Code Global Data": Overview

CoCd	Company		Country	Crcy	Langua
4510	US Company	Vancouver	CA	USD	EN
4520	Canadian 2 Company	Toronto	CA	CAD	EN
4600	Malaysia	Kuala Lumpur			EN
4700	Indonesia	Jakarta	ID		EN
4800	Philippines	Manila	PH	PHP	
5000	IDES Japan 5000	Tokyo	JP	JPY	JA
5100	IDES Singapore	Singapore	SG	SGD	EN
5200		okyo	JP	JPY	JA
5400		Amsterdam	NL	EUR	NL
54	XYZ Company bv	Amsterdam	NL	EUR	NL
5402	My New Company	Amsterdam	NL	EUR	NL
6000	IDES México, S.A. de C.V.	México DF	MX	MXN	ES
6001	Empresa México "A"	D.F.	MX	MXN	ES
6002	Empresa México "B"	Monterrey	MX	MXN	ES
6003	Empresa México **FM**	D.F.	MX	MXN	ES

Callouts:
- 3. Click icon or select F2 to see company code details
- 1. Scroll
- 2. Select company code

Figure 1.18: Assign global parameters to company code, step 4

Change View "Company Code Global Data": Details

Additional Data

Company Code	5402	My New Company	Amsterdam	
Country key	NL	Currency	EUR Language Key	NL

Accounting organization

Chart of Accts	INTL	Country Chart/Accts		
Company		FM Area		
Credit control area	1000	Fiscal Year Variant	K4	
Ext. co. code		Global CoCde		
Company code is productive	✓	VAT Registration No.	NL008209893B01	

Processing parameters

Document entry screen variant		☐ Business area fin. statements	
Field status variant	1000	✓ Propose fiscal year	
Pstng period variant	1000	✓ Define default value date	
Max. exchange rate deviation	10 %	☐ No forex rate diff. when clearing in LC	
Sample acct rules var.		☐ Tax base is net value	
Workflow variant		☐ Discount base is net value	
Inflation Method		✓ Financial Assets Mgmt active	
Crcy transl. for tax		☐ Purchase acct proc.	
CoCd -> CO Area		☐ JV Accounting Active	
Cost of sales accounting actv.		☐ Hedge request active	
✓ Negative Postings Permitted		☐ Enable amount split	
✓ Activate CM		☐ Tax Reporting Date Active	
☐ Manage Postg Period			

Figure 1.19: Assign global parameters to company code, step 5

Table view   Edit   Goto   Choose   Utilities

Change View "Company Code Global Data": Details

Additional Data

Field status variant	1000	☐ Propose fiscal year	
Pstng period variant	1000	☐ Define default value date	
Max. exchange rate deviation	10 %	☐ No forex rate diff. when clearing in l	
Sample acct rules var.		☐ Tax base is net value	
Workflow variant		☐ Discount base is net value	
Inflation Method		☐ Financial Assets Mgmt active	
Crcy transl. for tax		☐ Purchase acct proc.	
CoCd -> CO Area		☐ JV Accounting Active	

Data was saved   SAP   I68 (1) 850   sap01-205   INS

Figure 1.20: Assign global parameters to company code, step 6

Assign company code to controlling area

What is a controlling area?

The controlling area in SAP FI is an organizational unit that is a level above the company code. You can have many company codes assigned to a controlling area, but a company code can only be assigned to one controlling area. The controlling area provides the linkage between the FI module and the controlling (CO) module.

A discussion of the functionalities available with the CO module is not within scope of this book; however, because of a systemic requirement for a company code to be assigned to a controlling area, it must be mentioned. It is assumed that the IDES environment that you are working in already has a controlling area configured; only the assignment of company codes to the controlling area will be discussed.

Assign company code to controlling area

Just as you had done for creating a company code and assigning global parameters, in order to assign a company code to a controlling area, access the SAP REFERENCE IMG menu by following the steps below:

1. Type SPRO in the command field and then press ⌈Enter⌉. (Figure 1.21).

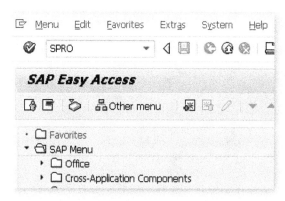

Figure 1.21: Assign company code to controlling area, step 1

2. Click on SAP REFERENCE IMG (Figure 1.22).

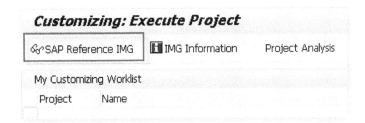

Figure 1.22: Assign company code to controlling area, step 2

3. From the SAP CUSTOMIZING IMPLEMENTATION GUIDE MENU, navigate to CONTROLLING • GENERAL CONTROLLING • ORGANIZATION • MAINTAIN CONTROLLING AREA (Figure 1.23).

4. Click ⊕ to execute the transaction.

5. Double click on MAINTAIN CONTROLLING AREA (Figure 1.24).

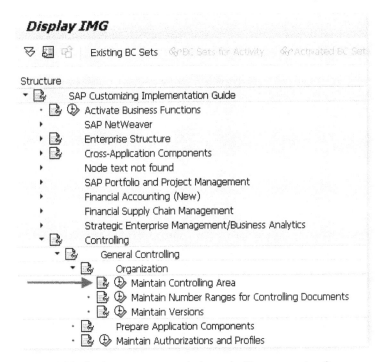

Figure 1.23: Assign company code to controlling area, step 3

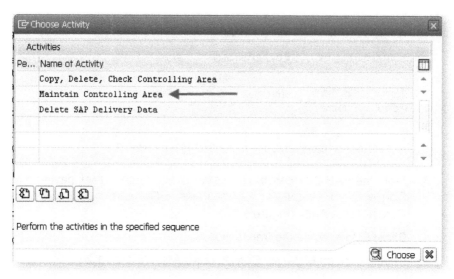

Figure 1.24: Assign company code to controlling area, step 5

A list of existing controlling areas are shown (Figure 1.25).

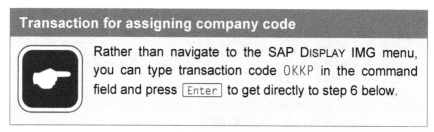

Transaction for assigning company code

Rather than navigate to the SAP DISPLAY IMG menu, you can type transaction code OKKP in the command field and press Enter to get directly to step 6 below.

6. From the list of controlling areas codes presented, scroll to the controlling area desired and select it by clicking on the box to the left. The controlling area will be highlighted. Next, double click on AS-SIGNMENT OF COMPANY CODE(S) in the left navigation pane.

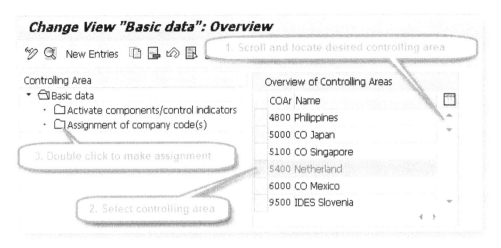

Figure 1.25: Assign company code to controlling area, step 6

7. With ASSIGNMENT OF COMPANY CODE(S) SELECTED, click on New Entries. (Figure 1.26).

8. Enter company code and press [Enter] (Figure 1.27)

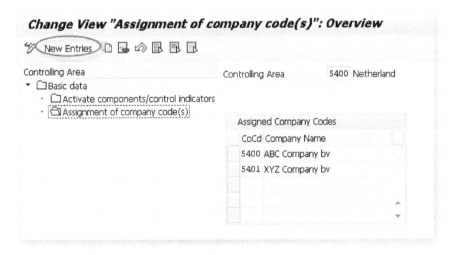

Figure 1.26: Assign company code to controlling area, step 7

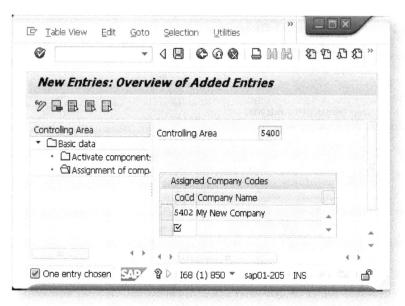

Figure 1.27: Assign company code to controlling area, step 8

9. Click the SAVE icon to save entries. Note the message returned that the "Data was saved" (Figure 1.28).

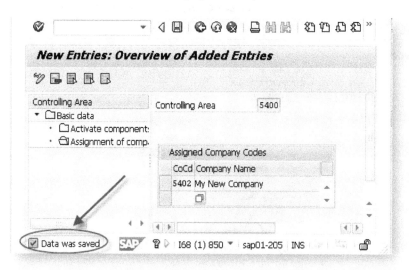

Figure 1.28: Assign company code to controlling area, step 9

Assign number ranges to documents

Each document in SAP FI is assigned a unique document number. The combination of document number, document year, and company code will provide a key used by SAP FI for locating documents for reporting or subsequent processing. Different number ranges can be defined in SAP FI for different document types. For example, customer invoices might use one range of document numbers while vendor invoices use another.

Before we can post transactions in a company code, number ranges must be assigned to the company code. The simplest way to assign number ranges is to copy the ranges from one company code to the newly created company code.

We will copy number ranges from company code 5401 to our newly created company code 5402:

1. Type SPRO in the command field and then press [Enter]. (Figure 1.29).

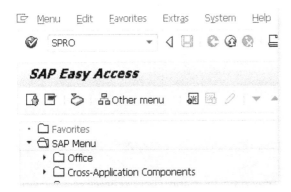

Figure 1.29: Assign number ranges to company code, step 1

2. Click on SAP REFERENCE IMG (Figure 1.30).

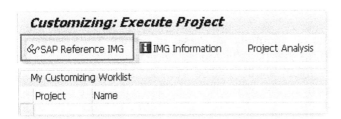

Figure 1.30: Assign number ranges to company code, step 2

31

3. From the SAP CUSTOMIZING IMPLEMENTATION GUIDE menu, navigate to: FINANCIAL ACCOUNTING (NEW) • FINANCIAL ACCOUNTING GLOBAL SETTINGS (NEW) • DOCUMENT • DOCUMENT NUMBER RANGES • DOCU- MENTS IN ENTRY VIEW • COPY TO COMPANY CODE (Figure 1.31).

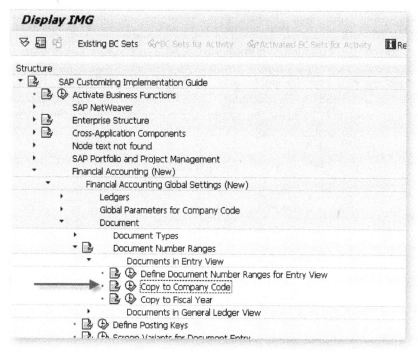

Figure 1.31: Assign number ranges to company code, step 3

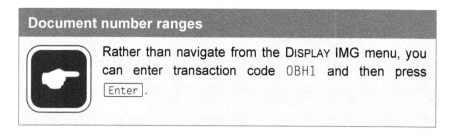

Document number ranges

Rather than navigate from the DISPLAY IMG menu, you can enter transaction code OBH1 and then press Enter.

4. SAP FI presents an informational message (Figure 1.32) pertaining to transports. Note that number ranges, though configured from the implementation guide, should not be transported from the develop- ment environment to the productive environment because they are likely already in use. (See the Preface, as well as Figure 1.10 to Fi- gure 1.12 for a discussion of transports). Access to changing number

ranges in the productive environment, however, will likely be limited to certain individuals. Click ENTER CONTINUE ✔️.

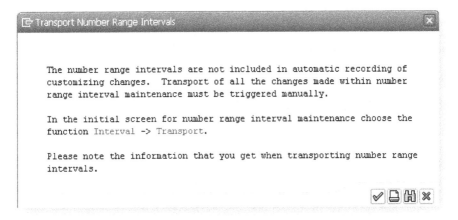

Figure 1.32: Assign number ranges to company code, step 4

5. Enter the source company code information and the target (destination) company code and then click EXECUTE ⊕ (Figure 1.33). Note in our example, we are copying two number ranges that have been set up in company code 5401 to our new company code 5402.

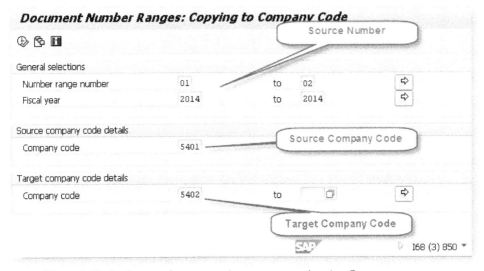

Figure 1.33: Assign number ranges to company code, step 5

6. SAP FI will provide another prompt to make sure you want to edit number ranges. Click YES to continue (Figure 1.34).

Figure 1.34: Assign number ranges to company code, step 6

7. A message is returned indicating the number ranges have been added (Figure 1.35). Click the BACK icon ☯ to return to the SAP CUSTOM-IZING IMPLEMENTATION GUIDE menu.

❷		▾ ◁ 🗏 ☯☯☯ 🗏🏦🏦 ☯☯☯☯ 🖾🖾 ☯🗊		

Document Number Ranges: Copying to Company Code

☯ ☯☯☯ ☯☯☯☯ ⊞ ▮ ◄ ◄ ► ►

Espresso Tutorial	Copy document number ranges to company code	Time 19:40:09	Date 09/20/2015
Heidelberg	Source company code 5401	RFNRIV10	Page 1

CoCd	No	Year	Status Text	Message Text
5402	01	2014	Interval added	
5402	02	2014	Interval added	

Figure 1.35: Assign number ranges to company code, step 7

The document-splitting functionality of the new GL is beyond the scope of this text; however, if you are operating in a new GL environment and if document splitting is active in the environment you are working in, you may need to deactivate splitting for the company codes you are creating in order to post transactions without the complete document splitting configuration (Figure 1.37).

1. To deactivate splitting, use SPRO to access the SAP CUSTOMIZING IMPLEMENTATION GUIDE menu and then navigate to FINANCIAL AC-COUNTING (NEW) • GENERAL LEDGER ACCOUNTING (NEW) • BUSINESS TRANSACTIONS • DOCUMENT SPLITTING • ACTIVATE DOCUMENT SPLIT-TING.

2. Select DEACTIVATION PER COMPANY CODE on the left panel (Figure 1.37). Scroll to the company code created and choose the inactive selection. Save by clicking the SAVE icon 🖫.

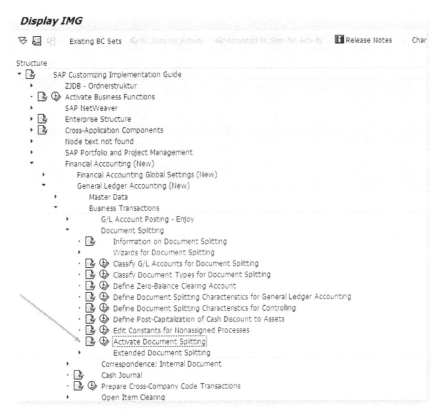

Figure 1.36: Deactivate document splitting, step 1

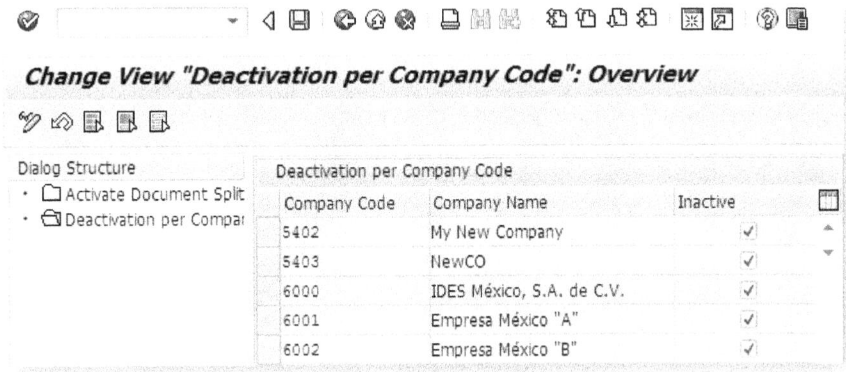

Figure 1.37: Deactivate document splitting, step 2

3. If prompted for a transport, follow the steps shown in Figure 1.10: Create company code, step 11 to Figure 1.12: Create company code, step 13.

You have now finished creating a company code and configuring all parameters necessary for posting transactions.

Display a company code

To display a company code, you can use SPRO to access the SAP CUSTOMIZING CONFIGURATION GUIDE menu and then navigate to ENTERPRISE STRUCTURE • DEFINITION • FINANCIAL ACCOUNTING • EDIT, COPY, DELETE, CHECK COMPANY CODE, or enter 0X02 in the command field and click the ENTER icon 🗸.

Double click on EDIT COMPANY CODE DATA as shown in Figure 1.4.

Click the CHANGE/DISPLAY icon ✏️ to switch to a display view. Note that the title bar will now read "Display View" instead of "Change View" as shown on the left side of Figure 1.38.

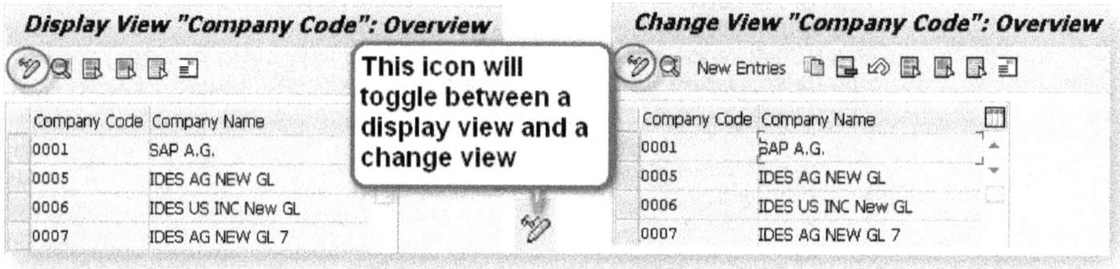

Figure 1.38: Switch to display view

From the list of company codes, scroll to a company code and click the DETAILS icon 🔍 (Figure 1.39).

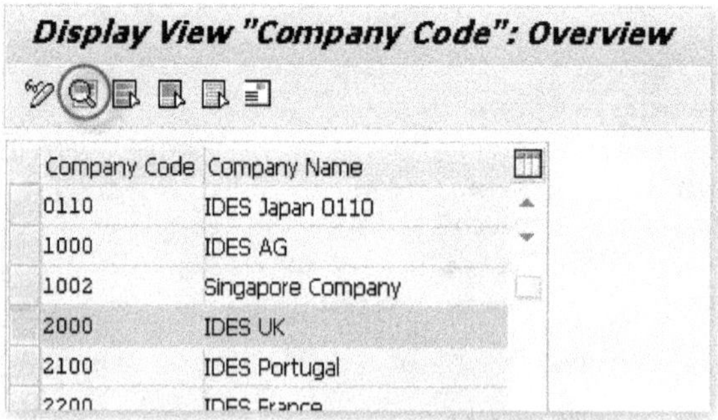

Figure 1.39: Select a company code to display

Detail information for the company code is displayed. Note that all text fields are not open for change in the display view (Figure 1.40).

Display View "Company Code": Details

Company Code	2000
Company Name	IDES UK

Additional data

City	London
Country	GB
Currency	GBP
Language	EN

Figure 1.40: Display company code

For address details, click the ADDRESS icon ▤.

Display global parameters

Similarly, you can display global parameters for any company code. From the SAP CUSTOMIZING IMPLEMENTATION GUIDE menu (SPRO) navigate to FINANCIAL ACCOUNTING (NEW) • FINANCIAL ACCOUNTING GLOBAL SETTINGS (NEW) • GLOBAL PARAMETERS FOR COMPANY CODE • ENTER GLOBAL PARAMETERS. Or type OBY6 in the command field and click the ENTER icon ✅.

Use the CHANGE/DISPLAY icon ✎ to switch to a display view. Next, scroll to a company code and click the DETAILS icon 🔍 (Figure 1.41).

Display View "Company Code Global Data": Overview

CoCd	Company Name	City	Country	Crcy	Langua
2100	IDES Portugal	Lisbon	PT	EUR	PT
2200	IDES France	Paris	FR	EUR	FR
2201	IDES France affiliate	Paris	FR	EUR	FR
2300	IDES España	Barcelona	ES	EUR	ES

Figure 1.41: Select display global parameters

Global parameters are displayed (Figure 1.42).

Display View "Company Code Global Data": Details

≡ Additional Data ◀ ▶ 🖨

Company Code	2201	IDES France affiliate		Paris		
Country key	FR	Currency	EUR	Language Key		FR

Accounting organization

Chart of Accts	CAFR	Country Chart/Accts	INT
Company	2201	FM Area	
Credit control area	1000	Fiscal Year Variant	K4
Ext. co. code	☐	Global CoCde	
Company code is productive	☐	VAT Registration No.	FR93341612695

Processing parameters

Document entry screen variant	2	☑ Business area fin. statements
Field status variant	2200	☑ Propose fiscal year
Pstng period variant	2200	☑ Define default value date
Max. exchange rate deviation	10 %	☐ No forex rate diff. when clearing in LC
Sample acct rules var.		☐ Tax base is net value
Workflow variant		☐ Discount base is net value
Inflation Method		☐ Financial Assets Mgmt active
Crcy transl. for tax	☐	☑ Purchase acct proc.
CoCd -> CO Area	☐	☐ JV Accounting Active
Cost of sales accounting actv.	2	☐ Hedge request active
☐ Negative Postings Permitted		☐ Enable amount split
☑ Activate CM		☐ Tax Reporting Date Active
☐ Manage Postg Period		

Figure 1.42: Display global parameters

1.3   Create a chart of accounts

When creating a company code, recall that we needed to assign a chart of accounts to the company code (See Figure 1.19). The chart of accounts is a collection of accounts. SAP FI contains sample charts of accounts and it is common for companies to copy a sample chart and edit it to meet the specific business requirements of the company. In our IDES environment, the chart INT has already been copied to INT1, and as we saw when we created our company code, chart INT1 was assigned to the company code (See Figure 1.19).

Copying a chart of accounts

Transaction code OBY7 can be used to copy a chart of accounts. Since the IDES environment already has a chart of accounts established, the details of this transaction are not covered in this text.

Extend the chart of accounts to a company code

Although chart INT1 has been assigned to the company code, accounts in the chart are not set up for use in the company code. Each account to be used in the company code must be "extended" to that company code. Transaction codes FSS0 and FS00 are often used by individuals responsible for account maintenance to extend individual accounts to a company code. However, it would take a significant amount of time to extend each account in a chart to a new company code. SAP FI provides a transaction that enables all of the accounts used in one company code to be extended to another.

This transaction is accessed from the SAP EASY ACCESS menu rather than from the SAP CUSTOMIZING IMPLEMENTATION GUIDE (SPRO) menu.

Navigate to the COMPARE COMPANY CODE menu option as follows from the SAP MENU:

ACCOUNTING • FINANCIAL ACCOUNTING • GENERAL LEDGER • MASTER RECORDS • G/L ACCOUNTS • COMPARE COMPANY CODE • FS15 – SEND (Figure 1.43).

Copy chart of accounts to a new company code

Rather than navigate to the transaction, you can type transaction code FS15 in the command field and press ⌜Enter⌝ to get directly to the screen for copying the chart of accounts.

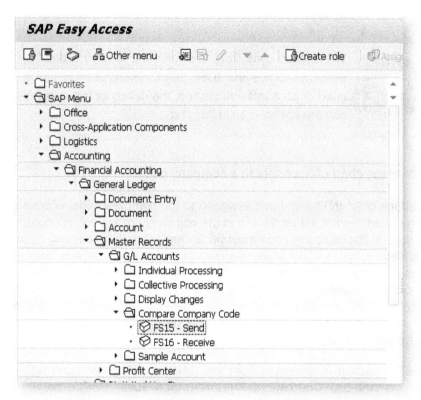

Figure 1.43: Copy chart of accounts to new company code

As shown in Figure 1.44, from the COPY GENERAL LEDGER ACCOUNT MASTER DATA: SEND screen, we can choose the source company code from which to copy a chart of accounts, as well as the target company code. We can choose to transfer any blocking indicators or deletion flags. We can update the master file immediately or process the update in a batch session. Processing in batch is beyond the scope of this text, so we will choose to update the file immediately. Although batch processing will not be used, a value is required in the BATCH INPUT SESSION NAME field.

We will first run the copy in a test mode by selecting ☐ Check file only to make sure that the copy will occur without errors. Finally, if desired, we could export the chart to a file which would then be imported to a different SAP FI environment with transaction code FS16. This is also beyond the scope of this text, so execute the transaction by clicking the EXECUTE icon ⊕ after the selection has been made as shown in Figure 1.44.

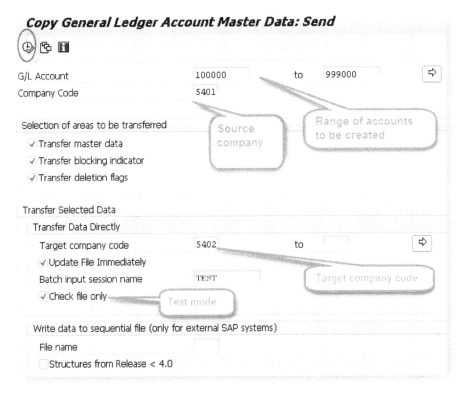

Figure 1.44: Copy chart of accounts from company 5401 to 5402

SAP FI returns with system messages advising of any errors to be corrected (Figure 1.45):

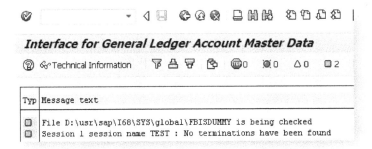

Figure 1.45: Copy chart of accounts, system messages

By clicking the BACK icon, we can display a list of accounts that will be created (Figure 1.46). Note that **Test Run** is indicated on the list.

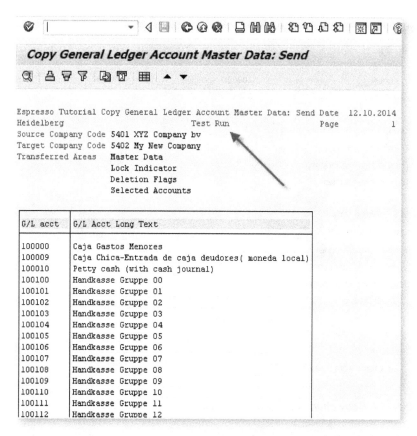

Figure 1.46: Copy chart of accounts, list to be created

Clicking the BACK icon 🔙 once more will return to the **FS15** screen. When ☐Check file only is deselected (Figure 1.44) and the EXECUTE icon ⊕ is clicked, the system copies the active chart of accounts in company code 5401 to 5402. If successful, a message returns indicating no messages (Figure 1.47).

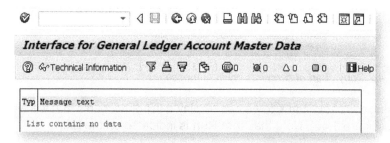

Figure 1.47: Copy chart of accounts, no messages

Clicking the BACK icon 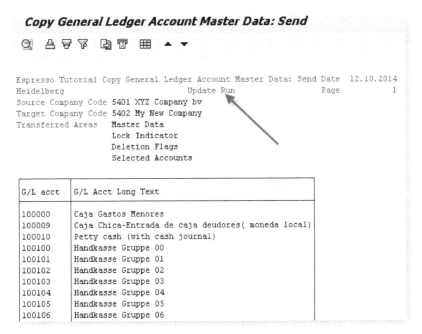 once again, results in a report of the accounts that were created, and **Update Run** is indicated (Figure 1.48).

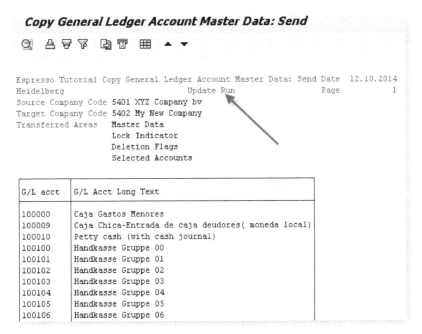

Figure 1.48: Copy chart of accounts, update run

1.4   Additional configuration items

Before users can post transactions to the new company code, some additional items may need to be configured.

Defining tolerance groups

Tolerance groups define maximum amounts for posting various transactions. Tolerance groups are defined for employees, general ledger accounts, and customer/vendor transactions. Tolerance groups are required before users can post transactions that involve clearing differences.

1.   To define the tolerance group for employees, from the SAP CUSTOM-IZING IMPLEMENTATION GUIDE menu navigate to FINANCIAL ACCOUNT-ING (NEW) • GENERAL LEDGER ACCOUNTING (NEW) • BUSINESS TRANS-ACTIONS • OPEN ITEM CLEARING • CLEARING DIFFERENCES • DEFINE TOLERANCE GROUPS FOR EMPLOYEES (Figure 1.49).

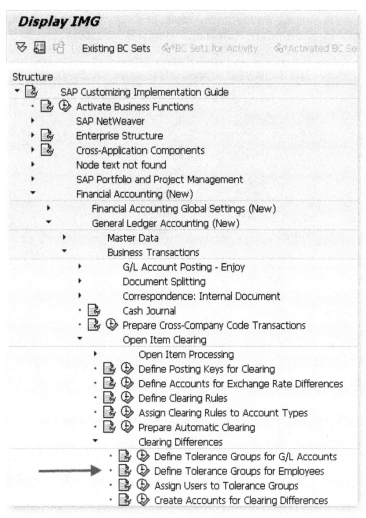

Figure 1.49: Define tolerance groups, step 1

Define tolerance group for employees

Rather than navigate to the SAP CUSTOMIZING IMPLE-
MENTATION GUIDE menu, you can type transaction code
OBA4 in the command field and press [Enter] to get
directly to the tolerance group for employees configuration screen.

2. From the overview screen (Figure 1.50) you can scroll to a company code and view settings for an existing company code. We will click New Entries because we will be defining tolerance groups for our sample company code 5402.

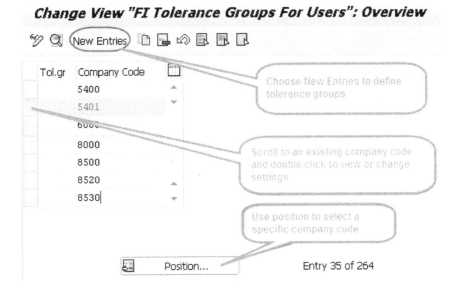

Figure 1.50: Define tolerance groups, step 2

3. Enter details for the tolerance group as shown in Figure 1.51.

    ▶ Enter a group only if you require different groups be assigned to different employees. In our example, we will assume all employees have the same tolerance levels.

    ▶ AMOUNT PER DOCUMENT represents the maximum document amount an employee is allowed to post.

    ▶ AMOUNT PER OPEN ITEM represents the maximum document amount for an open item account that an employee is allowed to post.

    ▶ CASH DISCOUNT PER LINE ITEM represents the maximum cash discount that may be recorded by an employee against an open item.

    ▶ PERMITTED PAYMENT DIFFERENCES represent the maximum differences when clearing that an employee will be allowed to post.

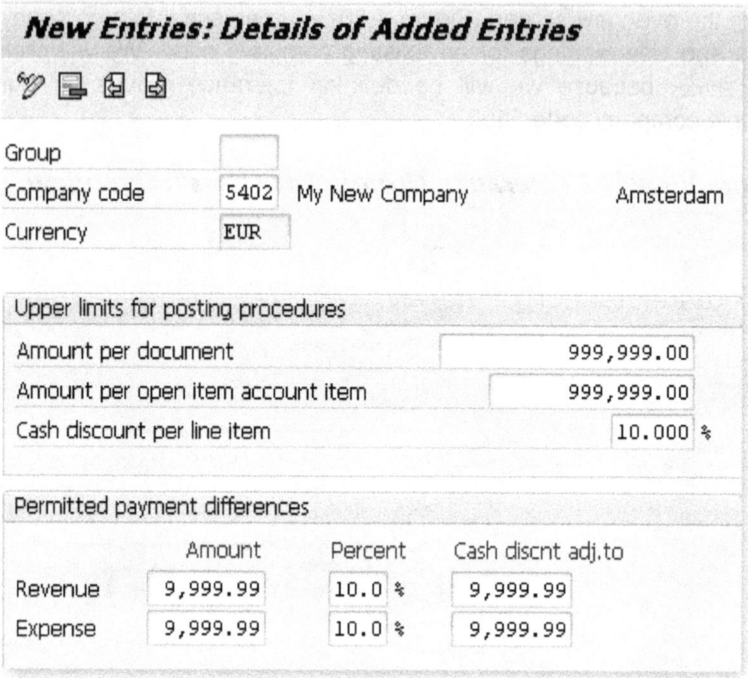

New Entries: Details of Added Entries

Group
Company code   5402   My New Company   Amsterdam
Currency   EUR

Upper limits for posting procedures

Amount per document	999,999.00
Amount per open item account item	999,999.00
Cash discount per line item	10.000 %

Permitted payment differences

	Amount	Percent	Cash discnt adj.to
Revenue	9,999.99	10.0 %	9,999.99
Expense	9,999.99	10.0 %	9,999.99

Figure 1.51: Define tolerance groups, step 3

4. Click the SAVE icon.

5. If prompted for a transport request, follow the steps shown in Figure 1.10 to Figure 1.12.

6. To define the tolerance group for customers/vendors, from the SAP CUSTOMIZING IMPLEMENTATION GUIDE menu navigate to FINANCIAL ACCOUNTING (NEW) • ACCOUNTS RECEIVABLE AND ACCOUNTS PAYABLE • BUSINESS TRANSACTIONS • OPEN ITEM CLEARING • CLEARING DIFFERENCES • DEFINE TOLERANCES FOR CUSTOMERS/VENDORS (Figure 1.52).

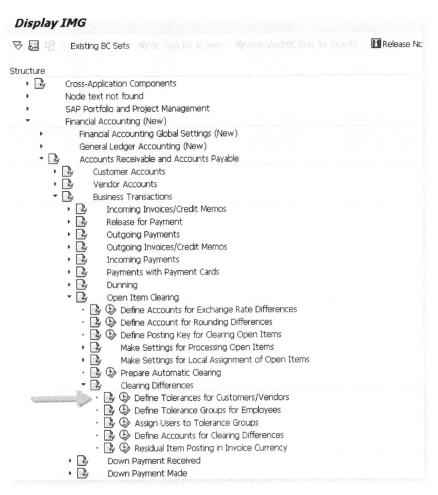

Figure 1.52: Define tolerance groups, step 6

Define tolerance group for customers/vendors

Rather than navigate to the transaction as shown above, you can type transaction code OBA3 in the command field and press [Enter] to get directly to the tolerance group [for customers/vendors] configuration screen.

7. As done with defining tolerance group for employees, click New Entries to define tolerance group for customers/vendors for our sample company code 5402 (Figure 1.53).

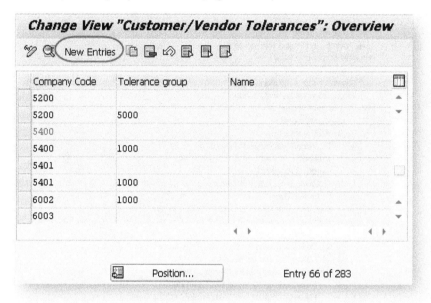

Figure 1.53: Define tolerance groups, step 7

8. It is not necessary to specify the detail settings, although they can be specified if desired. Rather, it is only necessary for a tolerance record to be established. In Figure 1.54, we are creating a tolerance record for company code 5402 customer/vendor transactions, but we are not entering any specific differences.

9. Click the SAVE icon 🖫 to save the record.

10. To define the tolerance groups for GL accounts, from the SAP Customizing Implementation Guide menu, navigate to Financial Accounting (New) • General Ledger Accounting (New) • Business Transactions • Open Item Clearing • Clearing Differences • Define Tolerance Groups for G/L Accounts (Figure 1.55)

Change View "Customer/Vendor Tolerances": Details

New Entries 🗋 🖫 ⟲ 🖬 🖬 🖳

Company Code 5402 My New Company   Amsterdam
Currency   EUR
Tolerance group

Specifications for Clearing Transactions

Grace days due date   Cash Discount Terms Displayed   0
Arrears Base Date

Permitted Payment Differences

	Amount	Percent	Adjust Discount By
Gain		%	
Loss		%	

Permitted Payment Differences for Automatic Write-Off (Function Code AD)

	Amount	Percent
Rev.		%
Expense		%

Specifications for Posting Residual Items from Payment Differences

☐ Payment Term from Invoice   Fixed payment term
☐ Only grant partial cash disc
Dunning key   ☐

Tolerances for Payment Advices

	Amount	Percent
Outst.receiv.from		%
Outst.payable from		%

Figure 1.54: Define tolerance groups, step 8

Define tolerance groups for GL accounts

Rather than navigate to the transaction, you can type transaction code OBA0 in the command field and press [Enter] to get directly to the tolerance group for GL accounts configuration screen.

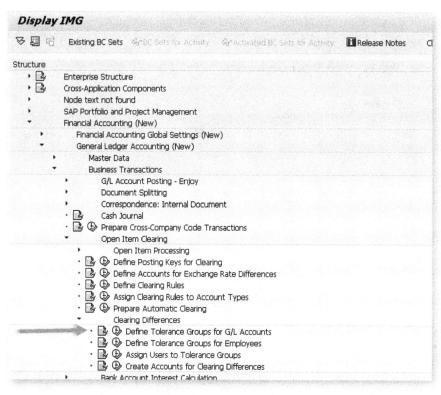

Figure 1.55: Define tolerance groups, step 10

11. As done with defining tolerance group for employees and customers/vendors, click New Entries to define a tolerance group for GL accounts for our sample company code 5402 (Figure 1.58).

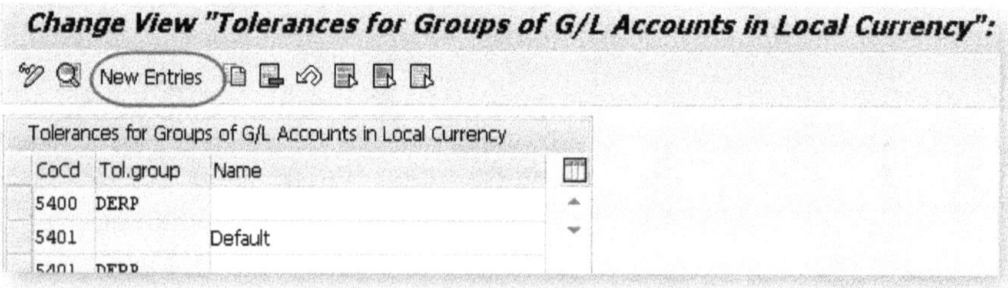

Figure 1.56: Define tolerance groups, step 11

12. It is not necessary to specify the detail settings, although they can be specified if desired. It is only necessary for a tolerance record to be established. In the example shown in Figure 1.57, we are creating a tolerance record for company code 5402 GL accounts, but we are not entering any specific differences.

Change View "Tolerances for Groups of G/L Accounts in Local Currency":

✓ New Entries 🗋 🖫 🗠 🖹 🖹 🖏

| Company Code | 5402 XYZ Company bv |
| Tolerance group | Default |

Tolerances for Groups of G/L Accounts in Local Curre

| Debit posting | | EUR | Percentage | | % |
| Credit posting | | EUR | Percentage | | % |

Figure 1.57: Define tolerance groups, step 12

13. Click the SAVE icon 🖫.

Posting periods

Posting period represents the accounting period in which the transaction will be recorded. A detailed discussion on posting period configuration is beyond the scope of this text; however, because the posting dates for accounting entries must fall within the posting period definitions, some discussion is warranted.

Posting periods are defined in "fiscal year variants." SAP FI delivers several fiscal year variants, the most common of which is "K4" which specifies a calendar year of 12 posting periods that match calendar months and 4 special periods that can be used for adjustments. You may recall (Figure 1.19) that variant "K4" was configured in the global parameters for our new company code.

Transaction code OB29 can be used to view or change fiscal year variants and the number of posting periods.

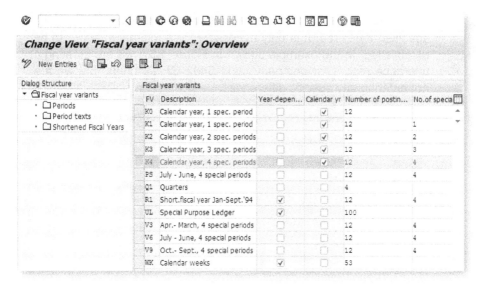

Figure 1.58: OB29 – Fiscal year variants

Posting period variants

A posting period variant controls which fiscal periods are open for transaction processing. After a period is closed, for example, you can lock it down so that no additional entries are made in that period. Because different company codes may have different requirements, the lock down is done by posting period variant. A company code can only be assigned one posting period variant; however several company codes can be assigned to one posting period variant.

Transaction code OB52 is used to open or close posting periods to activity for specific posting period variants. As shown in Figure 1.59, SAP FI provides a lot of flexibility with the control of open posting periods.

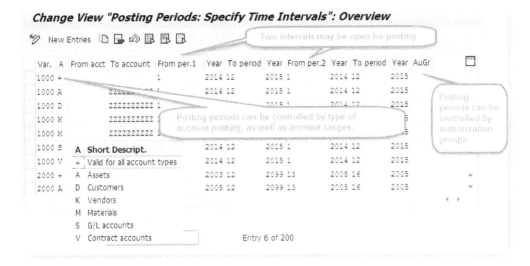

Figure 1.59: OB52, open or close posting periods

2 First steps in configuring accounts receivable

This chapter discusses the configuration required for managing accounts receivable.

SAP FI accounting transactions involving a customer, such as an invoice for a sales transaction or customer payment, are recorded in an accounts receivable subsidiary ledger, also known as a subledger. The integration functionality of the SAP FI system keeps the general ledger control account synchronized with the subledger account. The subledger account is also known as a reconciliation account. Some configuration is required in order to create customer master data, while other settings are necessary before transactions can be recorded.

2.1 Customer master data

2.1.1 Number ranges

For each customer record created, a customer number will be assigned. Customer numbers can be externally assigned, or assigned sequentially by the SAP FI system. Once number ranges are defined, the number ranges are assigned to customer groups.

Create a number range

Because the number range maintenance transaction is not part of the SAP EASY ACCESS menu, you must enter the SAP REFERENCE IMG menu by following the steps:

1. Type SPRO in the command field and then press ⌷Enter⌷ (Figure 2.1).

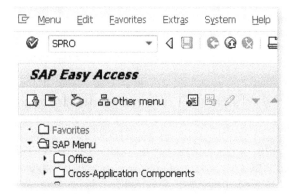

Figure 2.1: Create customer number ranges, step 1

2. Click on SAP REFERENCE IMG (Figure 2.2).

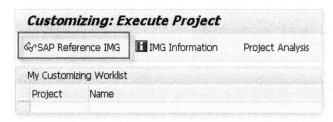

Figure 2.2: Create customer number ranges, step 2

3. Navigate to FINANCIAL ACCOUNTING (NEW) • ACCOUNTS RECEIVABLE AND ACCOUNTS PAYABLE • CUSTOMER ACCOUNTS • MASTER DATA • PREPARATIONS FOR CREATING CUSTOMER MASTER DATA • CREATE NUMBER RANGES FOR CUSTOMER ACCOUNTS (Figure 2.3).

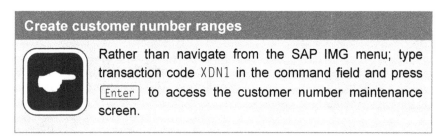

Create customer number ranges

Rather than navigate from the SAP IMG menu; type transaction code XDN1 in the command field and press Enter to access the customer number maintenance screen.

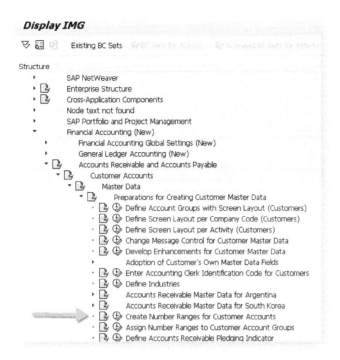

Figure 2.3: Create customer number ranges, step 3

4. Click the CHANGE INTERVALS button ☐ Intervals .

5. Click the INSERT LINE icon ☐.

6. Enter a number range and from and to values as shown in Figure 2.4 and click the SAVE icon ☐. For our example, create number range 54 which will internally assign numbers to customers.

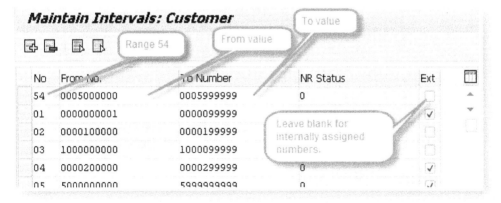

Figure 2.4: Create customer number range, step 6

7. SAP FI returns a message regarding number range transports (Figure 2.5). As before, the discussion of transports is beyond the scope of this text; however, it should be noted that special care should be taken when creating transports for number ranges in a productive environment. Many SAP FI projects maintain number ranges directly in the productive environment and this function is limited to very few individuals. Click ENTER CONTINUE ✔ to save the number ranges.

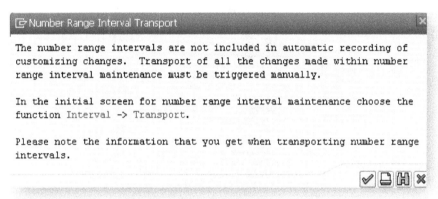

Figure 2.5: Create customer number range, step 7

8. Click the BACK icon ⬅ to return to the DISPLAY IMG menu.

Create customer account group

Customer account groups classify customers into various categories, for example: wholesale customers, consumers, etc. Separate "bill-to" and "ship-to" customers can be used in the SAP Sales and Distribution (SAP SD) module. A "one-time" customer account group is also common for certain types of customers. The fields that are required, optional, or suppressed in the customer master record are also designated by customer account group. The fields available are quite extensive.

1. At the DISPLAY IMG menu, navigate to FINANCIAL ACCOUNTING (NEW) • ACCOUNTS RECEIVABLE AND ACCOUNTS PAYABLE • CUSTOMER ACCOUNTS • MASTER DATA • PREPARATIONS FOR CREATING CUSTOMER MASTER DATA • DEFINE ACCOUNT GROUPS WITH SCREEN LAYOUT (CUSTOMERS) (Figure 2.6).

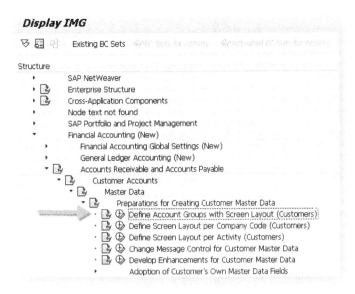

Figure 2.6: Define customer account groups, step 1

2. Rather than create a customer account group from scratch, copy an existing customer account group and edit settings as needed. From the list of customer account groups (Figure 2.7), select BILL-TO-PARTY and click the COPY AS icon.

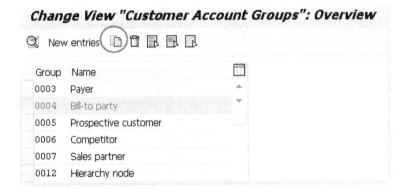

Figure 2.7: Define customer account groups, step 2

3. Enter the ACCOUNT GROUP (in this case account group 88) and a MEANING (description of the account group) and click the ENTER icon (Figure 2.8).

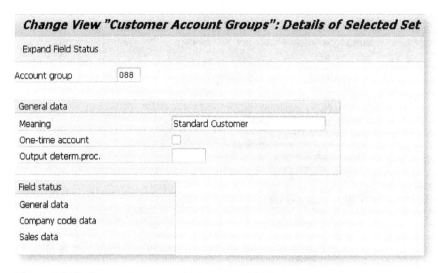

Figure 2.8: Define customer account group, step 3

4. With the new account group selected, click the DETAILS icon (Figure 2.9).

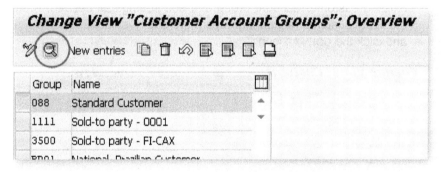

Figure 2.9: Define customer account group, step 4

5. With company code data selected, click EXPAND FIELD STATUS (Figure 2.10).

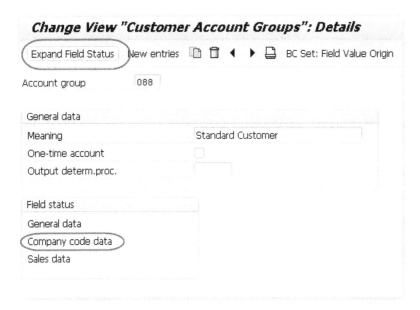

Figure 2.10: Define customer account group, step 5

6. With account management selected, click the DETAILS icon 🔍 (Figure 2.11).

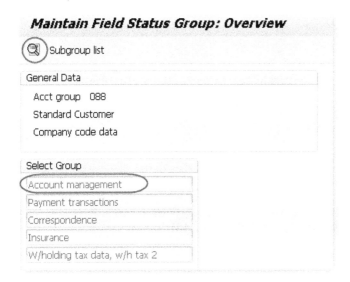

Figure 2.11: Define customer account group, step 6

7. Note that only the RECONCILIATION ACCOUNT field is selected as required (Figure 2.12). You may recall from the introduction to AR at the beginning of this chapter, that the reconciliation account is a general ledger account that contains the summary of transactions while the detail is held in the subledger. This selection should never be changed for customer account groups. To demonstrate changes, select "Suppress" for BUYING GROUP and PERSONNEL NUMBER and then click the SAVE icon 💾 to save your changes.

Maintain Field Status Group: Account management

📄 Field check

General Data				Page 1 / 1
Acct group 088				
Standard Customer				
Company code data				

Account management

	Suppress	Req. Entry	Opt. entry	Display
Reconciliation account	○	⊙	○	○
Cash management group	○	○	⊙	○
Previous account number	○	○	⊙	○
Sort key	○	○	⊙	○
Head office	○	○	⊙	○
Authorization	○	○	⊙	○
Preference indicator	○	○	⊙	○
Interest calculation	○	○	⊙	○
Buying Group	○	○	⊙	○
Personnel number	○	○	⊙	○
Release Group	⊙	○	○	○
Gross income tax	⊙	○	○	○
Value adjustment key	⊙	○	○	○

Figure 2.12: Define customer account group, step 7

8. When prompted for a transport request, enter a description and click the ENTER CONTINUE icon ✅ (Figure 2.13).

Figure 2.13: Define customer account group, step 8

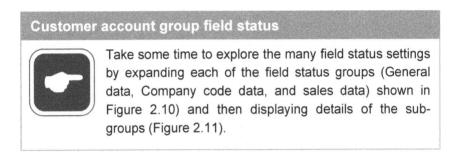

Take some time to explore the many field status settings by expanding each of the field status groups (General data, Company code data, and sales data) shown in Figure 2.10) and then displaying details of the sub-groups (Figure 2.11).

Assign number range to account group

Now that both the number ranges and account groups are created for the customer accounts, assign the number range to the account groups.

1. From the DISPLAY IMG menu navigate to FINANCIAL ACCOUNTING (NEW) • ACCOUNTS RECEIVABLE AND ACCOUNTS PAYABLE • CUSTOMER ACCOUNTS • MASTER DATA • PREPARATIONS FOR CREATING CUSTOMER MASTER DATA • ASSIGN NUMBER RANGES TO CUSTOMER ACCOUNT GROUPS (Figure 2.14).

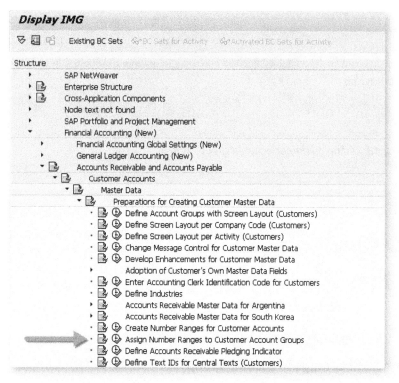

Figure 2.14: Assign number range to account group, step 1

2. Scroll to new account group 088 and enter "54" in the NUMBER RANGE column (Figure 2.15). Click the SAVE icon 🖫 to save the change.

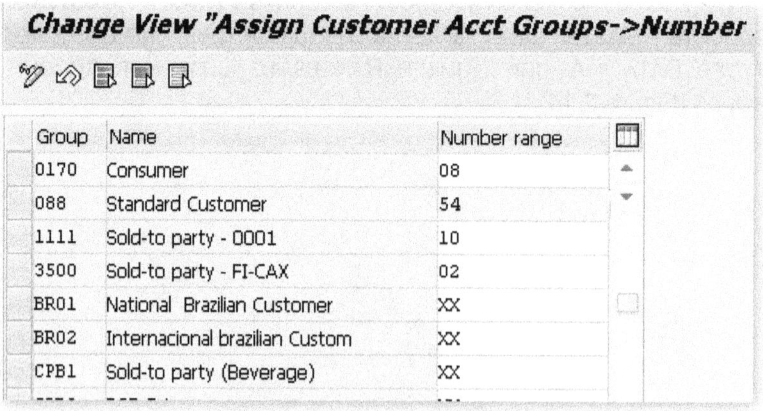

Figure 2.15: Assign number range to account group, step 2

2.1.2 Payment terms

Payment terms are an important attribute for processing accounts receivable transactions. Payment term definitions include the number of days from invoice date that a customer is allowed before payment is due. In addition, any discounts for making a payment prior to the due date is included in the payment terms record. Payment terms may be assigned to customer records or to transactions.

1. From the DISPLAY IMG menu navigate to FINANCIAL ACCOUNTING (NEW) • ACCOUNTS RECEIVABLE AND ACCOUNTS PAYABLE • BUSINESS TRANSACTIONS • OUTGOING INVOICES/CREDIT MEMOS • MAINTAIN TERMS OF PAYMENT (Figure 2.16).

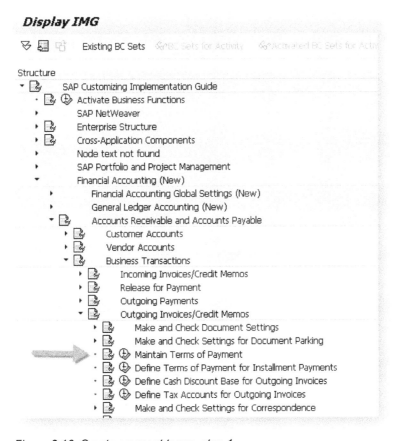

Figure 2.16: Create payment terms, step 1

2. Click New Entries (Figure 2.17).

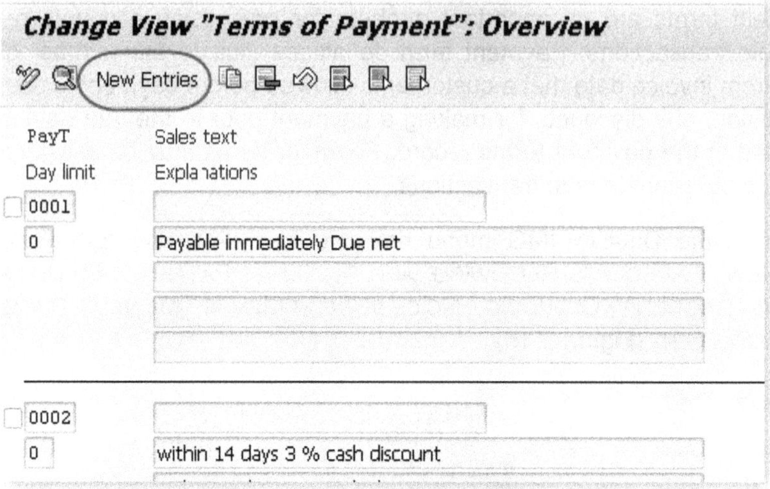

Figure 2.17: Create payment terms, step 2

3. Enter the payment terms information and click the SAVE icon 🖫 to save the new terms code (Figure 2.18).

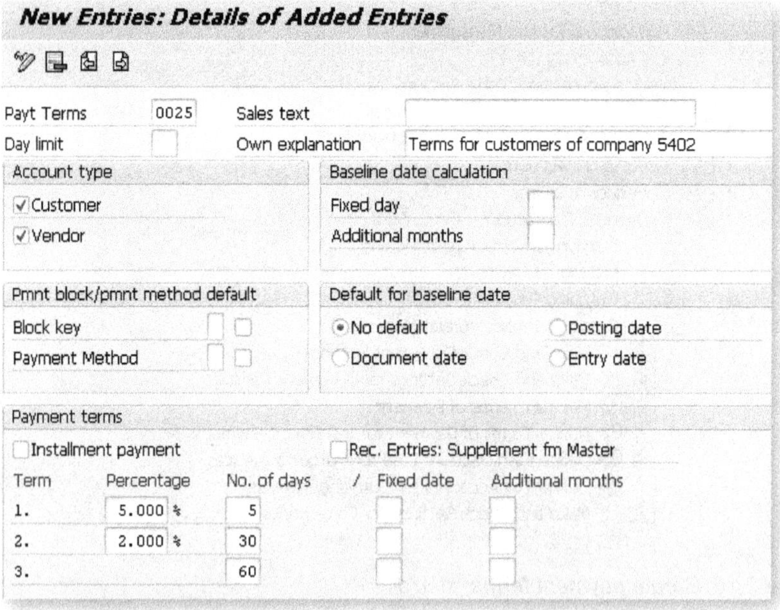

Figure 2.18: Create payment terms, step 3

4. When prompted for a transport request, enter a description and select the ENTER CONTINUE icon ✔ (Figure 2.19).

Figure 2.19: Create payment terms, step 4

In our example, we entered only the most common fields required which
also meet our specific requirements. Below is a list of the fields available
for payment terms.

Field	Description
Payt terms	4-character unique identifier for payment terms
Sales text	30-character explanation of terms to appear on invoices
Day limit	Used when terms are based upon the day of the month when the invoice is posted
Own explanation	Terms description
Account type	Select customer, vendor, or both to indicate which type of accounts these payment terms apply to
Fixed day	Used if the baseline date for terms should be overwritten by a specific calendar date. (Baseline date is the date from which the terms apply).
Additional months	Used if additional months are added to the calendar month of the baseline date
Block key	Results in a proposed block reason when goods issued (AR) or payment proposal is posted
Payment method	Indicates that the defined terms are applicable only if the specific payment method is used

Field	Description
Default for baseline date	Specifies which date is proposed for a baseline date when documents are created. If no default is selected, baseline date must be entered manually.
Installment payment	Used when invoice amount will have partial amounts with different due dates. When entering documents, system prompts for the breakdown.
Rec. entries	If this indicator is selected, and recurring entries are being posted, the terms will be derived from the customer/vendor master record rather than the original recurring document entry.
Term %	Percentage to be used for the discount
No. of days	Number of days from the baseline date for which the discount is allowed
Fixed date	Calendar date that the discount ends if baseline date is not used
Additional months	Used if additional months are added to the calendar month of the baseline date for the invoice to be eligible for discount

Table 2.1: Payment Terms

2.2 AR transactions

Before processing transactions in the AR subledger, there are two objects to configure: *reason codes* and *default account* assignments.

2.2.1 Reason codes

Oftentimes when a customer remits a payment for an invoice, there could be a difference in the payment as compared to the amount of the invoice. Perhaps there is a portion of the invoice that is disputed or an error in the amount being paid. Depending on the circumstances, you may want to charge the difference to a general ledger account or you may want to reflect the difference as a residual item on the customer's account. Reason codes are used to manage the disposition underpayments or over-payments on AR items.

Create two reason codes. One reason code will result in a charge to a ledger account, the other will result in a residual item posted to the customer's account.

1. To define reason codes, type SPRO in the command field and then press ⌈Enter⌋ (Figure 2.20).

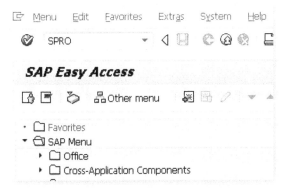

Figure 2.20: Define reason codes, step 1

2. Click on SAP REFERENCE IMG (Figure 2.21).

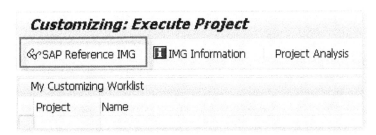

Figure 2.21: Define reason codes, step 2

3. Navigate to DEFINE REASON CODES: FINANCIAL ACCOUNTING (NEW) • ACCOUNTS RECEIVABLE AND ACCOUNTS PAYABLE • BUSINESS TRANSACTIONS • INCOMING PAYMENTS • INCOMING PAYMENTS GLOBAL SETTINGS • OVERPAYMENT/UNDERPAYMENT • DEFINE REASON CODES (Figure 2.22).

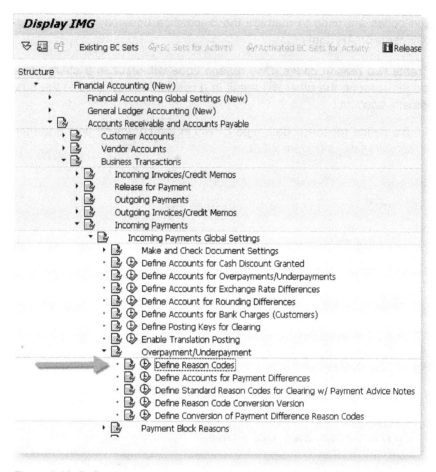

Figure 2.22: Define reason codes, step 3

Define reason codes

 Rather than navigate from the SAP EASY ACCESS menu; type transaction code OBBE in the command field and press [Enter] to access the define reason codes.

4. Enter the company code and click the ENTER CONTINUE icon ✓ (Figure 2.23).

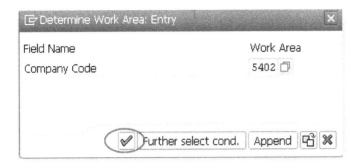

Figure 2.23: Define reason codes, step 4

5. Select New Entries (Figure 2.24).

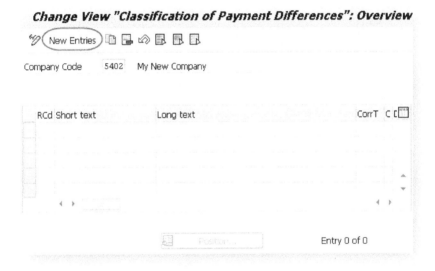

Figure 2.24: Define reason codes, step 5

6. Enter the applicable reason code data (see Table below) and click the SAVE icon 🖫 (Figure 2.25).

New Entries: Overview of Added Entries

Company Code   5402   My New Company

RCd	Short text	Long text	CorrT	C	D	Do not Copy...	Adv. Note Diff.
UAD	Unuath. Ded	Unauthorized deduction		☑		☐	☐
SPW	Short Pay	Short Pay Write off	☑	☐		☐	☐
				☐	☐	☐	☐
				☐	☐	☐	☐
				☐	☐	☐	☐
				☐	☐	☐	☐

Figure 2.25: Define reason codes, step 6

A description of the fields for reason code data is included in Table 2.2 below:

Field	Description
RCd	Three character unique code
Short text	Short description of reason code (20 chars)
Long text	Long description of reason code (40 chars)
Corr T	Correspondence type chosen from dropdown list. Correspondence types are used for generating letters to customers related to the payment differences.
C	The payment difference will be charged to a GL account (Refer to Default Account Assignments 2.2.2.)
D	The payment difference will be posted back to the customer account as a residual item (original item is cleared)
Do not copy text	The reason code text is not copied into the residual item, rather it must be entered manually.
Adv. Note Diff.	Tolerance differences are not considered when posting residual items.

Table 2.2: Reason code fields

2.2.2 Default account assignments

As noted in Chapter 2.2.1, there will be situations when the customer payment is greater or less than the invoice amount. The configuration of default account assignments can facilitate the handling of the payment differences. Additional postings to dispose of the differences can be automatic, saving time and providing for consistency and control. This section demonstrates some common account assignments related to customer payments: customer discounts, customer tolerances, and reason codes.

To access default account assignments, access the SAP IMG menu.

1. Type SPRO in the command field and press ⌈Enter⌉ (Figure 2.26).

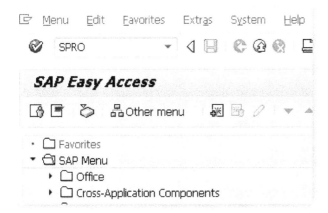

Figure 2.26: Default account assignments, step 1

2. Click on SAP REFERENCE IMG (Figure 2.27).

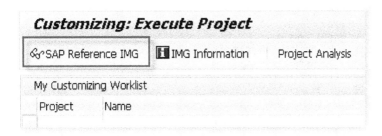

Figure 2.27: Default account assignments, step 2

3. Navigate to FINANCIAL ACCOUNTING (NEW) • ACCOUNTS RECEIVABLE AND ACCOUNTS PAYABLE • BUSINESS TRANSACTIONS • INCOMING PAYMENTS • INCOMING PAYMENTS GLOBAL SETTINGS (Figure 2.28).

Customer discounts

1. Navigate to FINANCIAL ACCOUNTING (NEW) • ACCOUNTS RECEIVABLE AND ACCOUNTS PAYABLE • BUSINESS TRANSACTIONS • INCOMING PAYMENTS • INCOMING PAYMENTS GLOBAL SETTINGS • DEFINE ACCOUNTS FOR CASH DISCOUNT GRANTED (Figure 2.28).

Define accounts for cash discounts

Rather than navigate from the SAP IMG menu, type transaction code OBXI in the command field and press Enter to access the defined reason codes.

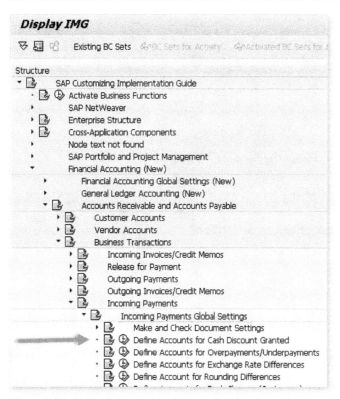

Figure 2.28: Default account assignments, step 1

2. Enter the CHART OF ACCOUNTS code and click the ENTER CONTINUE icon 🕑 (Figure 2.29).

Figure 2.29: Default account assignments, step 2

3. Enter the general ledger expense ACCOUNT number where discounts should be charged and click the SAVE icon 🖫 (Figure 2.30).

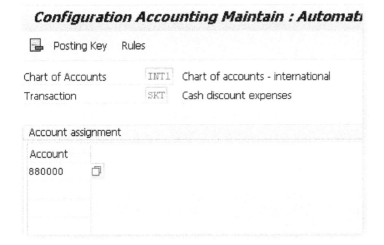

Figure 2.30: Default account assignment, step 3

4. When prompted for a transport request, enter a SHORT DESCRIPTION and click the ENTER CONTINUE icon ✔ (Figure 2.31).

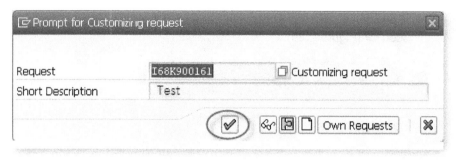

Figure 2.31: Default account assignment, step 4

5. SAP FI returns a message that "Changes have been made" (Figure 2.32). Select the BACK icon ✪ to return to the SAP IMG menu.

☑ Changes have been made

Figure 2.32: Default account assignment, step 5

Customer tolerances

In Chapter 1.4, we defined tolerance groups to enable posting of documents. However, as noted in Figure 1.54, at that time we chose only to create the tolerance groups without any detailed configuration. Let's go back to customer tolerances and configure tolerance amount and account determination. In our example, we want any payment differences that are the lower of 1% of the invoice amount or $10.00 to be automatically charged to general ledger account 889000 (Other Sales Deductions).

1. Navigate to the customer tolerance overview by following the menu path in Figure 1.52 or entering transaction code OBA3 in the command field and pressing ⌷Enter⌷.

2. Click the POSITION button at the bottom of the screen (Figure 2.33).

3. Enter the company code and click the ENTER CONTINUE icon ☑ (Figure 2.34).

4. With the COMPANY CODE line selected, click the DETAILS icon 🔍 (Figure 2.35).

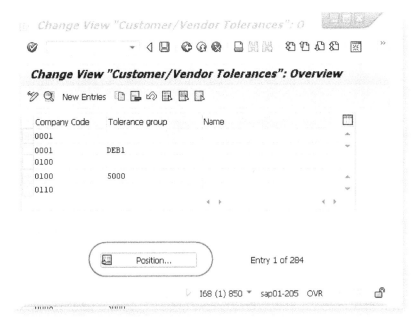

Figure 2.33: Customer tolerances step 2

Figure 2.34: Customer tolerances, step 3

Figure 2.35: Customer tolerances, step 4

5. Enter the tolerance amounts as shown in the permitted payment differences sections in Figure 2.36 and click the SAVE icon 🖫.

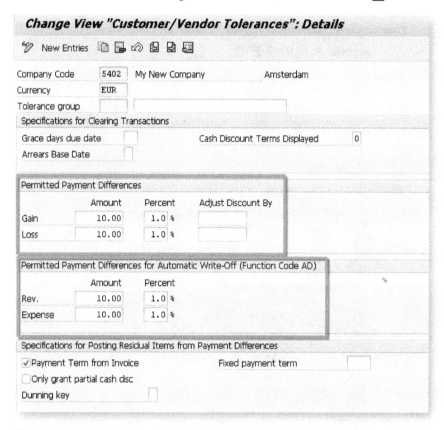

Figure 2.36: Customer tolerances, step 5

The account determination for customer tolerances will be configured with the same transaction as done for reason codes.

Reason codes

1. While in the SAP IMG menu, navigate to FINANCIAL ACCOUNTING (NEW) • ACCOUNTS RECEIVABLE AND ACCOUNTS PAYABLE • BUSINESS TRANSACTIONS • INCOMING PAYMENTS • INCOMING PAYMENTS GLOBAL SETTINGS • DEFINE ACCOUNTS FOR OVERPAYMENTS/ UNDERPAYMENTS (Figure 2.37).

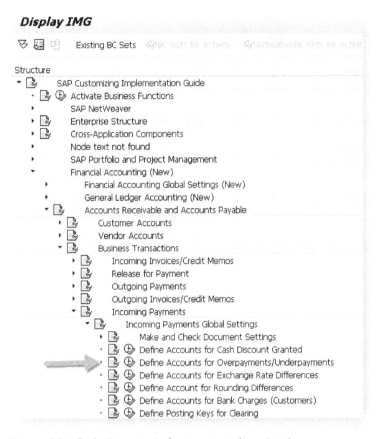

Figure 2.37: Default accounts for reason codes, step 1

Define accounts for reason codes

Rather than navigate from the SAP IMG menu; type transaction code OBXL in the command field and press [Enter] to access the define reason codes.

2. Enter the chart of accounts and click the ENTER CONTINUE icon ✓ (Figure 2.38).

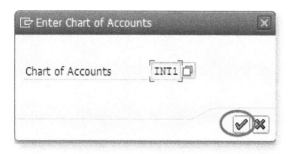

Figure 2.38: Default accounts, reason codes, step 2

3. Select the REASON CODE indicator and click the SAVE icon 💾 (Figure 2.39).

Figure 2.39: Default accounts, reason codes, step 3

4. Enter the reason code and GL account number (for the DEBIT and CREDIT columns) then click the SAVE icon 💾 (Figure 2.40). In the example below, account determination for reason code SPW, which was previously defined (Figure 2.25) is configured.

Configuration Accounting Maintain : Automatic Posts - Accounts

🗋 🗐 🖳 Posting Key   Rules

Chart of Accounts	INT1	Chart of accounts - international
Transaction	ZDI	Payment differences by reason

Account assignment

Reason code	Debit	Credit	
	889000	889000	
SPW	889000	889000	

Figure 2.40: Default accounts, reason codes, step 4

Automatic posts without reason code

One record for postings without reason codes should be maintained in order to enable the SAP function for automatically writing off tolerances.

5. When prompted for a transport request, enter a description and select the ENTER CONTINUE icon ✔ (Figure 2.41).

Figure 2.41: Default accounts, reason codes, step 5

6. SAP FI returns a message that the "Changes have been made" (Figure 2.42).

☑ Changes have been made

Figure 2.42: Default accounts, reason codes, step 6

Shortcut to default account assignments

SAP FI provides default account assignments for many different functions in addition to payment processing (taxes, asset management, etc.) FBKP is a shortcut transaction code that will enable you to configure the various account assignments from the same screen without navigating through the SAP IMG menu.

2.2.3 Define document number ranges for customer invoices

In most SAP FI implementations, invoices to customers will occur through the SD (sales and distribution) module, or via an interface from an external billing system. However, there are transactions which can be used in order to make a manual posting to a customer's account.

SAP FI contains several document types for customer transactions. These document types must be assigned number ranges and intervals must be assigned to the number ranges. Let's assign number ranges to all of the document types for customer transactions.

1.   Type SPRO in the command field and press ⎡Enter⎤ (Figure 2.43).

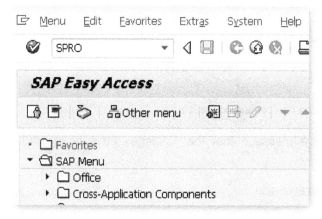

Figure 2.43: Customer document number ranges, step 1

2.   Click on SAP REFERENCE IMG (Figure 2.44).

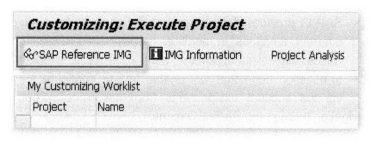

Figure 2.44: Customer document number ranges, step 2

3. From the SAP IMG menu, navigate to FINANCIAL ACCO UNTING (NEW) • FINANCIAL ACCOUNTING GLOBAL SETTINGS (NEW) • DOCUMENT • DOCU-MENT TYPES • DEFINE DOCUMENT TYPES FOR ENTRY VIEW (Figure 2.45).

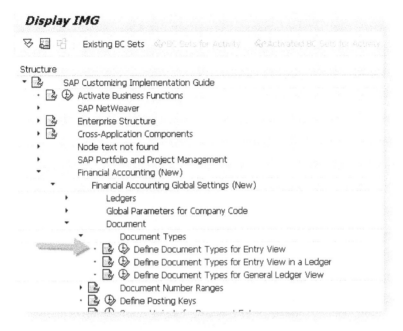

Figure 2.45: Customer document number ranges, step 3

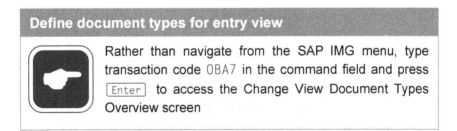

Define document types for entry view

Rather than navigate from the SAP IMG menu, type transaction code OBA7 in the command field and press Enter to access the Change View Document Types Overview screen

4. Scroll to the document types for customer documents. Select all of the customer documents by clicking the box to the left of each appli-cable document code and click the DETAILS icon (Figure 2.46).

5. From the detail view, note the number range, then click Number range information (Figure 2.47).

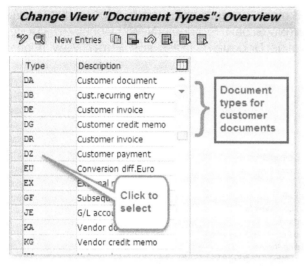

Figure 2.46: Customer document number ranges, step 4

Change View "Document Types": Details

New Entries

Document Type   DA   Customer document

Properties
Number range   16
Reverse DocumentType   AB
Authorization Group

Number range information

Account types allowed
☐ Assets
☑ Customer
☐ Vendor
☐ Material
☑ G/L account

Special usage
☐ Btch input only

Control data
☐ Net document type
☐ Cust/vend check
☑ Negative Postings Permitted
☐ Inter-company postgs
☐ Enter trading partner

Default values
Ex.rate type for forgn crncy docs

Required during document entry
☐ Reference number
☐ Document header text

Joint venture
Debit Rec.Indic
Rec.Ind. Credit

Figure 2.47: Customer document number ranges, step 5

6. Enter the company code and click ⌀ Intervals (Figure 2.48).

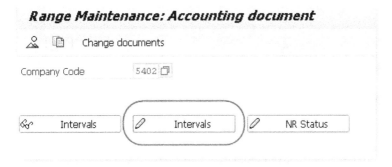

Figure 2.48: Customer document number ranges, step 6

7. Click the INSERT LINE icon 🗃 (Figure 2.49).

Interval Maintenance: Number Range Object Accounting docu

N..	Year	From No.	To Number	NR Status	Ext
01	2006	0100000000	0199999999	0	
01	2014	0100000000	0199999999	100000002	
02	2006	0200000000	0299999999	0	✓
02	2014	0200000000	0299999999	0	✓
X1	2014	9000000000	9100000000	9000000000	

Figure 2.49: Customer document number ranges, step 7

8. Enter the number range, the current year, and the intervals desired in the new row. Click the SAVE icon 🖫 to save the changes (Figure 2.50).

9. Click the ENTER CONTINUE icon ✅ when presented with a transport message concerning number ranges, then click the BACK icon 🔙 twice.

10. Click the NEXT ENTRY icon 🗊 (Figure 2.51).

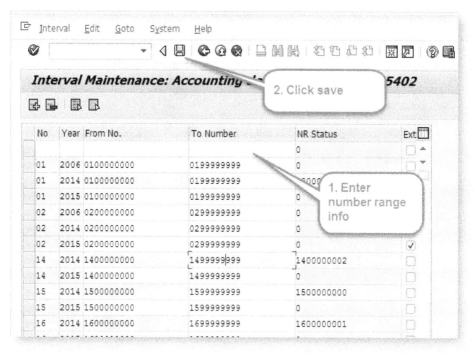

Figure 2.50: Customer document number ranges, step 8

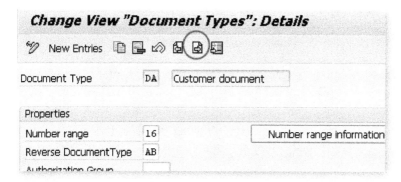

Figure 2.51: Customer document number ranges, step 10

11. Repeat steps 5 through 10 until all customer document types have number range intervals assigned (Figure 2.52).

Interval Maintenance: Number Range Object Accounting docum.

N..	Year	From No.	To Number	NR Status	Ext
01	2006	0100000000	0199999999	0	
01	2014	0100000000	0199999999	100000002	
02	2006	0200000000	0299999999	0	✓
02	2014	0200000000	0299999999	0	✓
14	2014	1400000000	1499999999	0	
16	2014	1600000000	1699999999	1600000001	
18	2014	1800000000	1899999999	1800000003	
29	2014	2900000000	2999999999	0	
X1	2014	9000000000	9100000000	9000000000	

Figure 2.52: Customer document number ranges, step 11

Define document number ranges for entry view

 Rather than navigate through each document type; if you know the number range that needs to be created or changed, enter the number range interval by accessing transaction code FBN1 or navigating from the DISPLAY IMG menu: FINANCIAL ACCOUNTING (NEW) • FINANCIAL ACCOUNTING GLOBAL SETTINGS (NEW) • DOCUMENT • DOCUMENT NUMBER RANGES • DOCUMENTS IN ENTRY VIEW • DEFINE DOCUMENT NUMBER RANGES FOR ENTRY VIEW.

With configuration for accounting completed, we can now use SAP FI transactions to post invoices to the customer account.

3 Getting started with accounts payable

This chapter discusses the configuration required for managing accounts payable.

3.1 What is SAP AP?

Most business enterprises make many purchases of goods and services daily from many vendors. Payments to the vendors are rarely made at the time of purchase. Based upon agreements with the vendors, payments may be made some time after the purchase; for example within 30 days. In addition, the payment amount may also vary, for example, if the company pays the vendor within 10 days, they may deduct a 1% discount.

The SAP Accounts Payable (SAP AP) module enables a company to record the expenses when incurred, monitor and settle the liabilities resulting from expenses, and facilitate the company's ability to take advantage of any discounts offered by vendors.

An SAP FI accounting transaction involving a purchase to be paid at a later date is recorded as a debit to an expense account and a credit to an accounts payable account. Similar to what was discussed in the accounts receivable chapter, a *subsidiary ledger* containing all details specific to payable accounts is used. Through the integration features of SAP FI, the subsidiary ledger will always agree to the total in the general ledger.

3.2 AP configuration

In addition to the creation of vendor master records, the AP module has additional configuration requirements in order to process payments to vendors. This section discusses the basic requirements for creating house banks and configuring a payment program.

3.2.1   House bank

A house bank is the bank used in a company code for banking transactions. Banks are set up with a bank key, usually the *SWIFT* code. SWIFT stands for Society for World Interbank Financial Telecommunication. However, in the United States some companies opt to use the American Bankers Association (ABA) number.

Because the house bank creation transaction is not part of the SAP EASY ACCESS menu, you must enter the SAP REFERENCE IMG menu.

1.   Type SPRO in the command field and then press Enter (Figure 3.1).

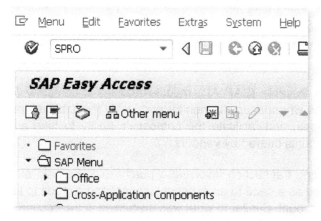

Figure 3.1: Create house bank, step 1

2.   Click on SAP REFERENCE IMG (Figure 3.2).

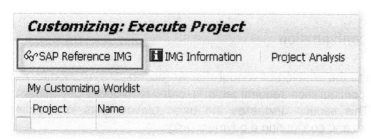

Figure 3.2: Create house bank, step 2

3. From the SAP CUSTOMIZING IMPLEMENTATION GUIDE menu, navigate to FINANCIAL ACCOUNTING (NEW) • BANK ACCOUNTING • BANK ACCOUNTS • DEFINE HOUSE BANKS (Figure 3.3).

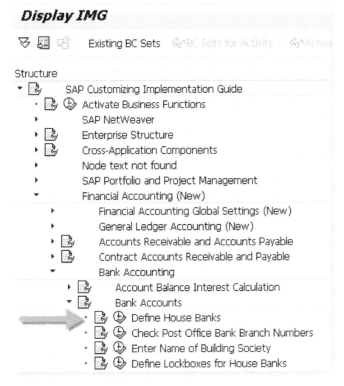

Figure 3.3: Create house bank, step 3

Create house bank

Rather than navigate through the SAP CUSTOMIZING IMPLEMENTATION GUIDE menu, you can type transaction code FI12 in the command field and press Enter .

---

4. Enter the applicable company code, 5402, and click the ENTER CONTINUE icon ✅ (Figure 3.4).

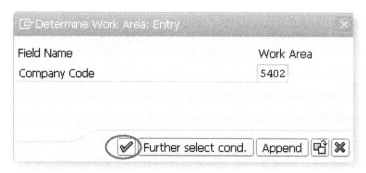

Figure 3.4: Create house bank, step 4

5. With HOUSE BANKS selected in the navigation panel on the left, click New Entries (Figure 3.5).

Figure 3.5: Create house bank, step 5

6. Enter a house bank code (any 5-character code desired for referring to the house bank) and the basic information required for the bank and then click ⬜ Create (Figure 3.6).

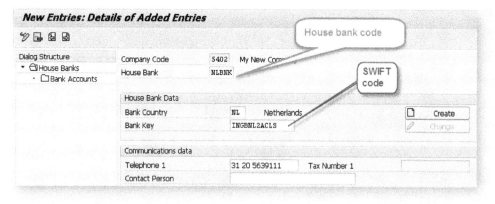

Figure 3.6: Create house bank, step 6

Length of bank key

 The length of the bank key in your environment may not allow the SWIFT code to be used. To change the length of the bank key, execute transaction code OY17 and change the length for each country code as needed.

7. Enter applicable details in the ADDRESS and CONTROL DATA sections and click the ENTER CONTINUE icon ✅ (Figure 4.7). The SWIFT/BIC field can be populated with the SWIFT code or with a BIC (Bank Identifier Code). These are codes used throughougt the world for automatic payment. The bank number is a unique identification key for a bank. Generally, the company's treasury department determines which codes to use.

Bank Data	
Bank Country	NL
Bank Key	INGBNL2ACLS
Address	
Bank name	ING Groep N.V.
Region	:
Street	Bijlmerplein 888
City	1102 MG Amsterdam
Bank Branch	Amsterdamse Poort
Control data	
SWIFT/BIC	INGBNL2ACLS
Bank group	
☐ Postbank Acct	
Bank number	54020001

Figure 3.7: Create house bank, step 7

8. Click the SAVE icon 💾. If prompted for a transport request, enter a description and click the ENTER CONTINUE icon ✅. Click the BACK icon ↩.

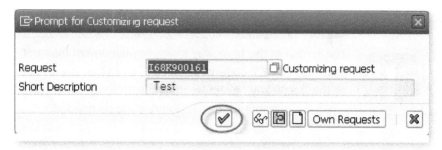

Figure 3.8: Create house bank, step 8

9. To assign a bank account and general ledger to the house bank, with the new house bank selected, double click on the BANK ACCOUNTS field (Figure 3.9).

Figure 3.9: Create house bank, step 9

10. Click New Entries (Figure 3.10).

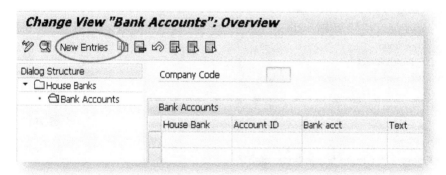

Figure 3.10: Create house bank, step 10

11. Enter a bank account ID and description. Then in the BANK ACCOUNT DATA section, enter a bank account number, the G/L account where transactions should be recorded, and the currency of the account. Click the SAVE icon 🖫 (Figure 3.11). If prompted for a transport request, enter a description and click the ENTER CONTINUE icon ✅. Click the BACK icon ⬅.

Figure 3.11: Create house bank, step 11

Country field checks

 Valid bank account numbers will be required depending on your SAP environment configuration. Consult with your treasury department for appropriate formats, if needed. To overcome any error messages regarding formats while you are in a development or test environment, use transaction code OY17 and deselect the country field checks for bank data.

3.2.2 Payment program

Configuration of the payment program is required in order for vendors to be paid. There are many steps involved in the configuration, these include:

▶ Setting up a company code as a paying company code

▶ Establishing parameters for the paying company code

▶ Setting up which payment methods can be used by a particular country

▶ Setting up which payment methods can be used by a specific company code

▶ Configuring bank determination for payment transactions

The items above represent the minimal configuration required in order to process payments in SAP FI. Many additional configuration settings can be made which will facilitate cash and liquidity management. However, this functionality is part of the SAP Financial Supply Chain Management (SAP FSCM) module which is beyond the scope of this text.

Configure only the check payment method for our examples. All of the configuration steps are performed from the SAP CUSTOMIZING IMPLEMENTATION GUIDE menu. Follow the steps shown in Figure 3.1 and Figure 3.2 to access the SAP IMG menu.

Set up all company codes for payment transactions

This step is necessary in order for company code 5402 to process payments in the SAP FI system.

1. From the SAP CUSTOMIZING IMPLEMENTATION GUIDE menu, navigate to FINANCIAL ACCOUNTING (NEW) • ACCOUNTS RECEIVABLE AND ACCOUNTS PAYABLE • BUSINESS TRANSACTIONS • OUTGOING PAYMENTS • AUTOMATIC OUTGOING PAYMENTS • PAYMENT METHOD/BANK SELECTION FOR PAYMENT PROGRAM • SET UP ALL COMPANY CODES FOR PAYMENT TRANSACTIONS (Figure 3.12).

2. Scroll to the company code you are working with and select it with a double click; or, as in the example, where the company code does not appear, click New Entries (Figure 3.13).

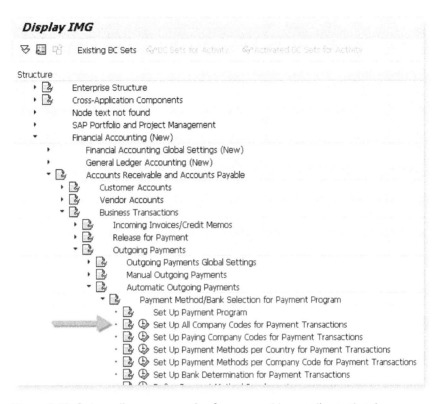

Figure 3.12: Set up all company codes for payment transactions, step 1

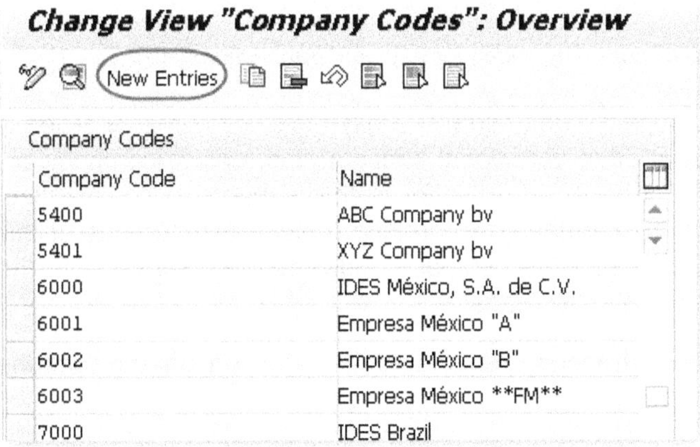

Figure 3.13: Set up all company codes for payment transactions, step 2

3. Enter company code 5402 in both SENDING COMPANY CODE and PAY-ING COMPANY CODE fields, then click the SAVE icon 💾 (Figure 3.14).

New Entries: Details of Added Entries

Company Code   5402 My New Company   ✍ Paying company code

Control data

Sending company code	5402	My New Company
Paying company code	5402	My New Company ℹ️
☐ Separate payment per business area		
☐ Pyt meth suppl.		

Cash discount and tolerances

Tolerance days for payable	
Outgoing pmnt with cash disc.from	‰
☐ Max.cash discount	

Vendors

Sp. G/L transactions to be paid	
Sp. G/L trans. for exception list	

Customers

Sp. G/L transactions to be paid	
Sp. G/L trans. for exception list	

Figure 3.14: Set up all company codes for payment transactions, step 3

In SAP FI, one company code can make payments for items recorded in a different company code. Additional configuration for intercompany accounting would be required in order for such payments to be recorded. The discussion of intercompany accounting is beyond the scope of this text. We will assume that the company code involved will be both the sending and paying company code.

4. If prompted for a transport request, enter a description and click the ENTER CONTINUE icon ✅ as shown in Figure 3.8.

Set up paying company code for payment transactions

This step provides specific details about payments processed from company code 5402 such as minimum payment amounts and forms to be used.

1. From the SAP CUSTOMIZING IMPLEMENTATION GUIDE menu, navigate to FINANCIAL ACCOUNTING (NEW) • ACCOUNTS RECEIVABLE AND ACCOUNTS PAYABLE • BUSINESS TRANSACTIONS • OUTGOING PAYMENTS • AUTOMATIC OUTGOING PAYMENTS • PAYMENT METHOD/BANK SELECTION FOR PAYMENT PROGRAM • SET UP PAYING COMPANY CODES FOR PAYMENT TRANSACTIONS (Figure 3.15).

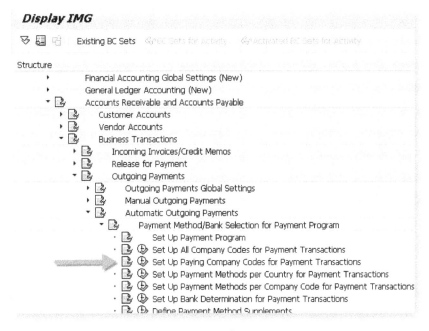

Figure 3.15: Set up paying company code for payment transactions, step 1

2. Scroll to the company code you are working with and select it with a double click; or, as in the example, where the company code does not appear, click New Entries (Figure 3.16).

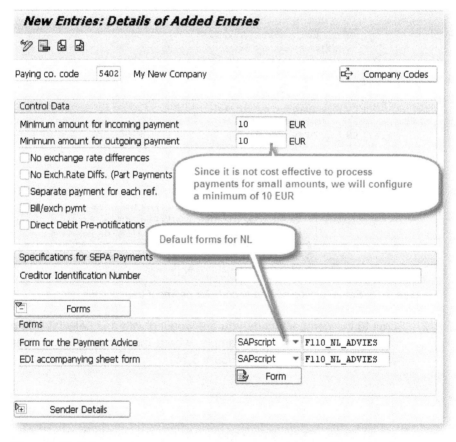

Figure 3.16: Set up paying company code for payment transactions, step 2

Figure 3.17: Set up paying company code for payment transactions, step 3

3. Enter the selections and click the SAVE icon ▣ (Figure 3.17). If prompted for a transport request, enter a description and click the ENTER CONTINUE icon ✅ as shown in Figure 3.8. Note that the discussion of forms is beyond the scope of this text. The company treasury department would work with SAP technical resources to determine the forms that would be appropriate for each company code.

Set up payment methods per country

There are many methods of making payments (checks, ACH, wire transfer, etc.). This step establishes the payment methods available for a particular country.

1. From the SAP CUSTOMIZING IMPLEMENTATION GUIDE menu, navigate to FINANCIAL ACCOUNTING (NEW) • ACCOUNTS RECEIVABLE AND ACCOUNTS PAYABLE • BUSINESS TRANSACTIONS • OUTGOING PAYMENTS • AUTOMATIC OUTGOING PAYMENTS • PAYMENT METHOD/BANK SELECTION FOR PAYMENT PROGRAM • SET UP PAYMENT METHODS PER COUNTRY FOR PAYMENT TRANSACTIONS (Figure 3.18).

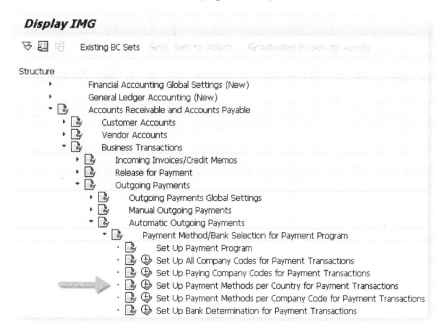

Figure 3.18: Set up payment methods per country, step 1

2. The standard SAP FI system is delivered with common payment methods and corresponding forms defined for each country. Therefore, your environment likely already has payment methods configured. If not, you may have to set them up. In Figure 3.19, the environment shown on the top already has a check method configured for Netherlands (NL). In this case, select the check method and click the DETAILS icon 🔍 to view the set-up or make any changes. The environment shown on the bottom does not have a check method. Click New Entries to create a check method.

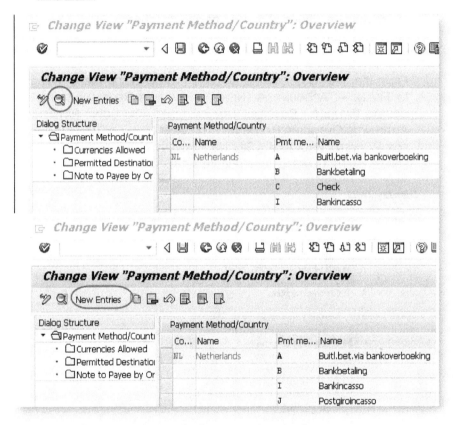

Figure 3.19: Set up payment methods per country, step 2

3. In Figure 3.20, the payment method for checks has already been set up. If any changes are desired, make sure you click the CHANGE/DIS-PLAY icon to enter change mode; make any desired changes and then click the SAVE icon. If you click New Entries, make the appropriate selections, and then click the SAVE icon to create your new payment method record. If prompted for a transport request, enter a description and click the ENTER CONTINUE icon as shown in Figure 3.8.

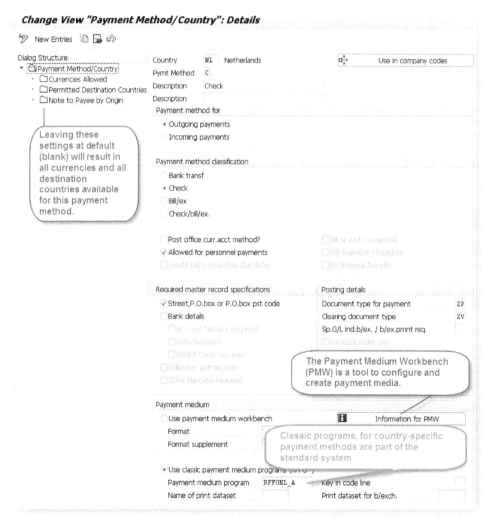

Figure 3.20: Set up payment methods per country, step 3

Set up payment method per company code

This step establishes the payment methods available from company code 5402. Set up only check payments.

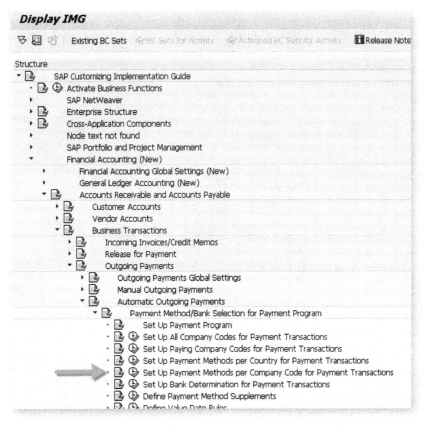

Figure 3.21: Set up payment methods per company code, step 1

1. From the SAP CUSTOMIZING IMPLEMENTATION GUIDE menu, navigate to FINANCIAL ACCOUNTING (NEW) • ACCOUNTS RECEIVABLE AND ACCOUNTS PAYABLE • BUSINESS TRANSACTIONS • OUTGOING PAYMENTS • AUTOMATIC OUTGOING PAYMENTS • PAYMENT METHOD/BANK SELECTION FOR PAYMENT PROGRAM • SET UP PAYMENT METHODS PER COMPANY CODE FOR PAYMENT TRANSACTIONS (Figure 3.21).

2. Scroll to locate the company code. If payment methods have already been established for the company code, click the DETAILS icon 🔍. If any changes are desired, click the CHANGE/DISPLAY icon 🖉 to enter change mode. Make any desired changes and then click the SAVE icon 🖫. In Figure 3.22, payment methods have not been established for company code 5402, so click New Entries.

3. Enter company code payment information and then click the SAVE icon 🖫 to create your new payment method record (Figure 3.23). If prompted for a transport request, enter a description and click the ENTER CONTINUE icon ✅ as shown in Figure 3.8.

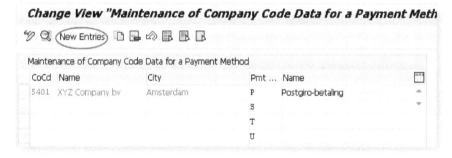

Figure 3.22: Set up payment methods per company code, step 2

105

Paying co. code 5402   My New Company   ✂   Pymt meth. in ctry
Pymt Method C   Check

Amount limits

Minimum amount	10.00	EUR
Maximum amount	250,000.00	EUR
Distribution amnt		EUR

Grouping of items

☐ Single payment for marked item
☐ Payment per due day
☐ Extended Individual Payment

Foreign payments/foreign currency payments

☑ Foreign business partner allowed
☑ Foreign currency allowed
☑ Cust/vendor bank abroad allowed?

Bank selection control

◉ No optimization
○ Optimize by bank group
○ Optimize by postal code

☲ Form Data

Use dropdown to select delivered or custom forms for checks.

Forms

Form for the Payment Medium	SAPscript ▾	F110_PRENUM_CHCK
Next form	SAPscript ▾	

Chose to display form details.

🗋 Form

Drawer on the form

My New Company
Surinamestratt 27
2585 GJ Den Haag NL

Sorting of the

Correspondence
Line items

☲ Pyt adv.ctrl

Payment advice note control

Note to payee lines on the form

○ restricted to   1 Rows
◉ None
○ as many as req

Advice notes in all instances

There is no note to payee line on the payment medium. Instead, a payment advice note is always created. This contains all the information about the purpose of the payment.

You can, for example, use this facility for bills of exchange.

Payment advice output according to no. of lines

○ Pymt adv. after ... lines
◉ Always pyt adv
○ NoPytAdv

Figure 3.23: Set up payment methods per company code, step 3

Set up bank determination for payment transactions

This step involves configuring multiple properties that will be used by the payment program for selecting the bank to be used for payments.

1. From the SAP CUSTOMIZING IMPLEMENTATION GUIDE menu, navigate to FINANCIAL ACCOUNTING (NEW) • ACCOUNTS RECEIVABLE AND AC-COUNTS PAYABLE • BUSINESS TRANSACTIONS • OUTGOING PAYMENTS • AUTOMATIC OUTGOING PAYMENTS • PAYMENT METHOD/BANK SELECTION FOR PAYMENT PROGRAM • SET UP BANK DETERMINATION FOR PAYMENT TRANSACTIONS (Figure 3.24).

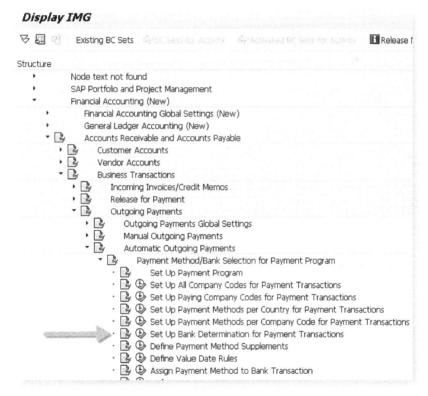

Figure 3.24: Set up bank determination for payment transactions, step 1

2. Scroll to company code 5402 and double click on the first property – RANKING ORDER (Figure 3.25). Ranking order is used to select the bank accounts that will be used in processing a payment run. It will be referenced only after any other selection control, such as choosing banks by postal code of vendor payment address. Note that in Figure 3.23, we selected NO OPTIMIZATION under BANK SELECTION

CONTROL. In the example, the ranking order configured here determines the bank to be used for payments.

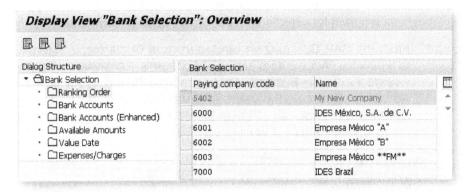

Figure 3.25: Set up bank determination for payment transactions, step 2

3. Click New Entries (Figure 3.26).

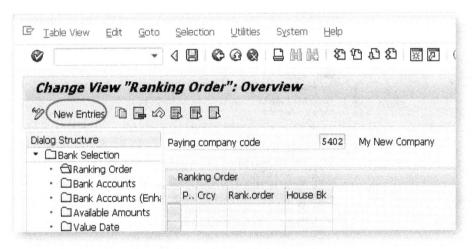

Figure 3.26: Set up bank determination for payment transactions, step 3

4. Enter records for each payment method (Figure 3.27). For company code 5402, we have only set up "C", check payment method, and one house bank. Therefore only one record is required. Click the SAVE icon 🖫 to save the record. If prompted for a transport request, enter a description and select the ENTER CONTINUE icon 🕢 as shown in Figure 3.8.

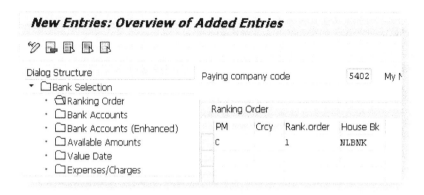

Figure 3.27: Set up bank determination for payment transactions, step 4

5. Double click on the BANK ACCOUNTS property and click New Entries (Figure 3.28).

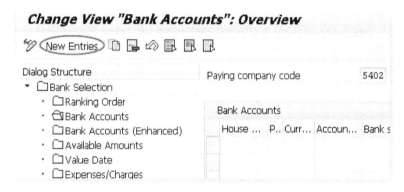

Figure 3.28: Set up bank determination for payment transactions, step 5

6. Enter a bank account ID and bank subaccount for the house bank and click the SAVE icon 🖫 (Figure 3.29).

New Entries: Overview of Added Entries

Dialog Structure
*   ▼ ☐ Bank Selection
    *   ☐ Ranking Order
    *   🖻 Bank Accounts
    *   ☐ Bank Accounts (Enh;
    *   ☐ Available Amounts
    *   ☐ Value Date
    *   ☐ Expenses/Charges

Paying company code   5402   My New Company

Bank Accounts

House ...	P..	Curr...	Accoun...	Bank subaccount	Charge ind	Bu...
NLBNK	C	EUR	1000	110002		
			☑	☑		
			☑	☑		

Figure 3.29: Set up bank determination for payment transactions, step 6

7. Double click on the AVAILABLE AMOUNTS field and click New Entries (Figure 3.30).

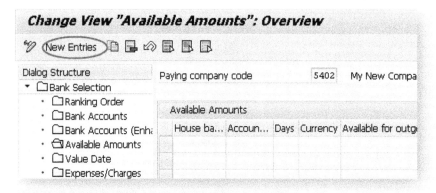

Figure 3.30: Set up bank determination for payment transactions, step 7

8. Enter the maximum amounts for outgoing and incoming payments for our house bank (Figure 3.30) and click the SAVE icon.

Figure 3.31: Set up bank determination for payment transactions, step 8

3.2.3 Vendor master data

Before creating vendor master data, you need to configure the SAP FI environment for vendor groups and number ranges.

Create number ranges for vendors

Because the number range maintenance transaction is not part of the SAP EASY ACCESS menu, you must enter the SAP REFERENCE IMG menu by following the steps below.

1. Type SPRO in the command field and then press ⌐Enter⌐ (Figure 3.32).

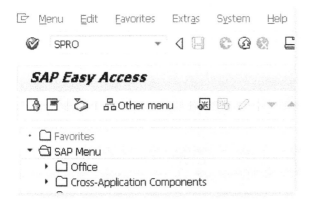

Figure 3.32: Create vendor number ranges, step 1

2. Click on SAP REFERENCE IMG (Figure 3.33).

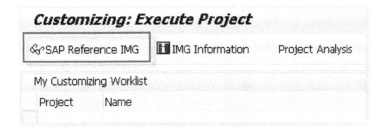

Figure 3.33: Create vendor number ranges, step 2

3. Navigate to FINANCIAL ACCOUNTING (NEW) • ACCOUNTS RECEIVABLE AND ACCOUNTS PAYABLE • VENDOR ACCOUNTS • MASTER DATA • PREPARATIONS FOR CREATING VENDOR MASTER DATA • CREATE NUMBER RANGES FOR VENDOR ACCOUNTS (Figure 3.34).

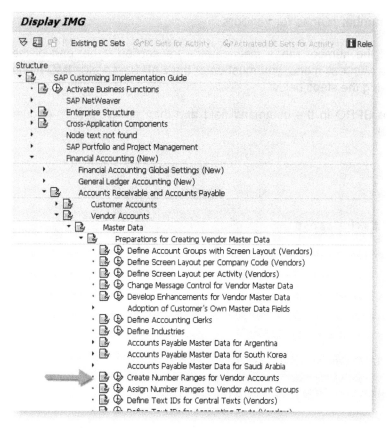

Figure 3.34: Create vendor number ranges, step 3

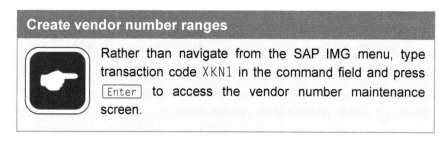

Create vendor number ranges

Rather than navigate from the SAP IMG menu, type transaction code XKN1 in the command field and press [Enter] to access the vendor number maintenance screen.

4. Click the CHANGE INTERVALS button [Intervals].

5. Click the INSERT LINE icon.

6. Enter a number range and from and to values and click the SAVE icon. As shown in Figure 3.35, create number range 64 which will internally assign numbers to vendors.

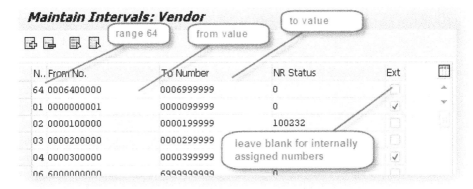

Figure 3.35: Create vendor number ranges, step 6

7. SAP FI returns a message regarding number range transports (Figure 3.36). As before, the discussion of transports is beyond the scope of this text; however, it should be noted that special care should be taken when creating transports for number ranges in a productive environment. Many SAP FI projects maintain number ranges directly in the productive environment and this function is limited to very few individuals. Click ENTER CONTINUE ✅ to save the number ranges.

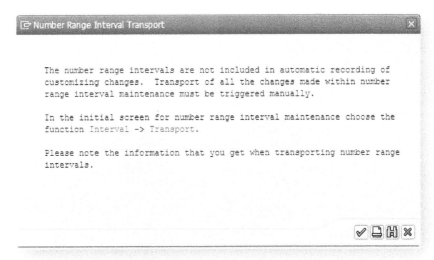

Figure 3.36: Create vendor number ranges, step 7

8. Click the BACK icon ⊖ to return to the DISPLAY IMG menu.

Define vendor account groups

Vendor account groups classify vendors into various categories, for example: suppliers, national vendors, forwarding agents, etc. The fields that are required, optional, or suppressed in the vendor master record are also designated by vendor account group. As you will see, the fields available are quite extensive.

1. At the DISPLAY IMG menu, navigate to FINANCIAL ACCOUNTING (NEW) • ACCOUNTS RECEIVABLE AND ACCOUNTS PAYABLE • VENDOR ACCOUNTS • MASTER DATA • PREPARATIONS FOR CREATING VENDOR MASTER DATA • DEFINE ACCOUNT GROUPS WITH SCREEN LAYOUT (VENDORS) (Figure 3.37).

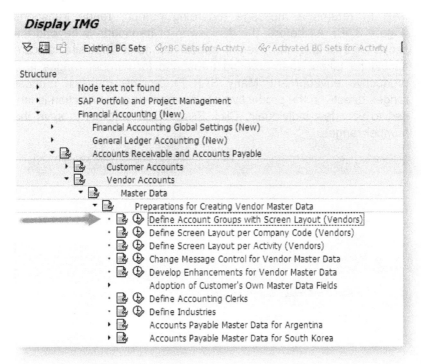

Figure 3.37: Define vendor account group, step 1

2. Rather than create a vendor account group from scratch, copy an existing vendor account group and edit any settings as needed. From the list of vendor account groups (Figure 3.38), select the line "0001 Vendors" and click the COPY AS icon.

Figure 3.38: Define vendor account groups, step 2

3. Enter account group number 0008 and a free-form description into the MEANING field and click ENTER ✅ (Figure 3.39).

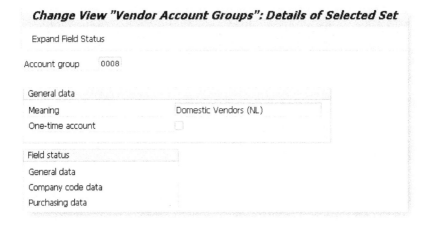

Figure 3.39: Define vendor account group, step 3

4. With the new account group selected, click the DETAILS icon 🔍 (Figure 3.40).

Figure 3.40: Define vendor account group, step 4

115

5. With COMPANY CODE DATA selected, click EXPAND FIELD STATUS (Figure 3.41).

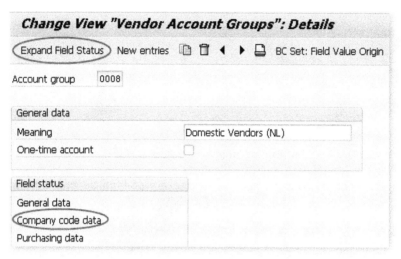

Figure 3.41: Define vendor account group, step 5

6. With ACCOUNT MANAGEMENT selected, click the DETAILS icon (Figure 3.42).

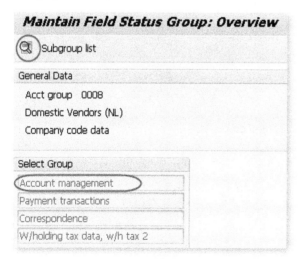

Figure 3.42: Define vendor account group, step 6

7. In Figure 3.43, note that two fields are marked as required: RECON-CILIATION ACCOUNT and CASH MANAGEMENT GROUP. As noted in the introduction to AP in section 3.1, the reconciliation account is a general ledger account that contains the summary of transactions while the detail is held in the subledger. This selection should never be changed for vendor account groups. To demonstrate changes, select suppress for PERSONNEL NUMBER, and opt entry for CASH MANAGE-MENT GROUP, then click the SAVE icon 💾.

Maintain Field Status Group: Account management

📄 Field check

General Data   Page   1 / 1

Acct group   0008
Domestic Vendors (NL)
Company code data

Account management

	Suppress	Req. Entry	Opt. entry	Display
Reconciliation account	○	◉	○	○
Cash management group	○	◉	○	○
Previous account number	○	○	◉	○
Sort key	○	○	◉	○
Head office	○	○	◉	○
Authorization	○	○	◉	○
Preference indicator	○	○	◉	○
Minority indicator	○	○	◉	○
Withholding tax code (1)	○	○	◉	○
Wthld.tax exempt., wthld.tax 1	○	○	◉	○
Interest calculation	○	○	◉	○
Withh.tax cat.,exemp.reason(1)	○	○	◉	○
Withholding Tax Country	○	○	◉	○
Personnel number	○	○	◉	○
Release Group	○	○	◉	○
Gross income tax	○	○	◉	○

Figure 3.43: Define vendor account group, step 7

Cash management group required

If the SAP Financial Supply Chain Management functionality is active in your environment, the cash management group may still be required when creating vendors.

To complete the setting to have cash management group optional, from the DISPLAY IMG menu, navigate to FINANCIAL SUPPLY CHAIN MANAGEMENT • CASH AND LIQUIDITY MANAGEMENT • CASH MANAGEMENT • MASTER DATA • SUBLEDGER ACCOUNTS • VENDOR CONTROL • DEFINE TRANSACTION-DEPENDENT FIELD SELECTION (VENDOR).

Next select CREATE VENDOR (ACCOUNTING) and click the DETAILS icon ⊞.

Choose the COMPANY CODE DATA field status group and expand field status by selecting EXPAND FIELD STATUS. Double-click on the AC-COUNT MANAGEMENT sub-group, then mark CASH MANAGEMENT GROUP as optional and click the SAVE icon 💾.

8. When prompted for a transport request, enter a description and click the ENTER CONTINUE icon ✅ as shown in Figure 3.8.

Vendor account group field status

Take some time to explore the many field status settings under GENERAL DATA and PURCHASING DATA shown under FIELD STATUS in Figure 3.41, by selecting sub-groups (Figure 3.42) and choosing the DETAILS icon ⊞.

Assign number range to account group

Now that both the number ranges and account groups are created for the customer accounts, assign the number range to the account group.

1. From the DISPLAY IMG menu navigate to FINANCIAL ACCOUNTING (NEW) • ACCOUNTS RECEIVABLE AND ACCOUNTS PAYABLE • VENDOR AC-COUNTS • MASTER DATA • PREPARATIONS FOR CREATING VENDOR MAS-TER DATA • ASSIGN NUMBER RANGES TO VENDOR ACCOUNT GROUPS (Figure 3.44).

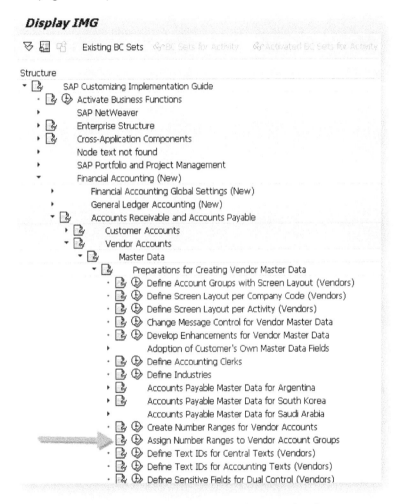

Figure 3.44: Assign number range to account group, step 1

2. Scroll to new account group 0008 and enter 64 in the NUMBER RANGE column (Figure 3.45). Click the SAVE icon to save the change.

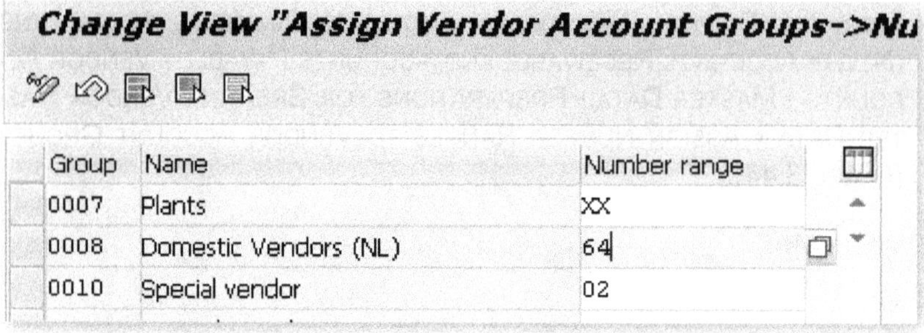

Figure 3.45: Assign number range to account group, step 2

3. When prompted for a transport request, enter a description and click the ENTER CONTINUE icon ☑ as shown in Figure 3.8.

4 Advanced topic: SAP tables

4.1 What are SAP tables?

As we have seen from our introduction to SAP GL, AR, and AP, there is plenty of information being stored in the SAP FI system. As in any database system, the information is stored across hundreds of tables which are accessed by the SAP FI programs.

Each table has a unique table name and is comprised of various fields which contain data. For example, the table named T001 contains information about company codes. The fields in the table include a company code number, address, currency, country code, etc. Each of the fields are also given technical names which are shown later in this chapter

SAP FI uses tables not only to contain master data records and transaction records, but also to house all of the configuration information that is used when executing programs. During your SAP FI experience, there are oftentimes when you might want to view the structure of a table or even the records contained in the table. When working with technical resources to design custom reports or processes, referencing the tables and fields is imperative.

Occasionally, you might encounter an error message that references a table. The ability to look at the table structure or data might help with resolving the error. Finally, there may be occasions when, rather than executing a standard SAP FI report, you wish to look at data directly in a table. This chapter will identify common tables used in SAP FI, AR, and AP and demonstrate how to view the contents of the tables.

Restrictions on table access

 In many SAP FI environments, access to view tables outside of the SAP FI standard programs is limited to technical resources or "power users." Although there may be access to tables using the tools described in this chapter, you should never make entries directly to tables outside of prescribed SAP FI programs.

4.1.1   How to find a table name

It is not difficult to find the name of a field and the table that contains the field when you are in an SAP FI transaction. As shown in Figure 4.1, accessed from transaction code **FD03**, the display shows various fields related to a customer master record.

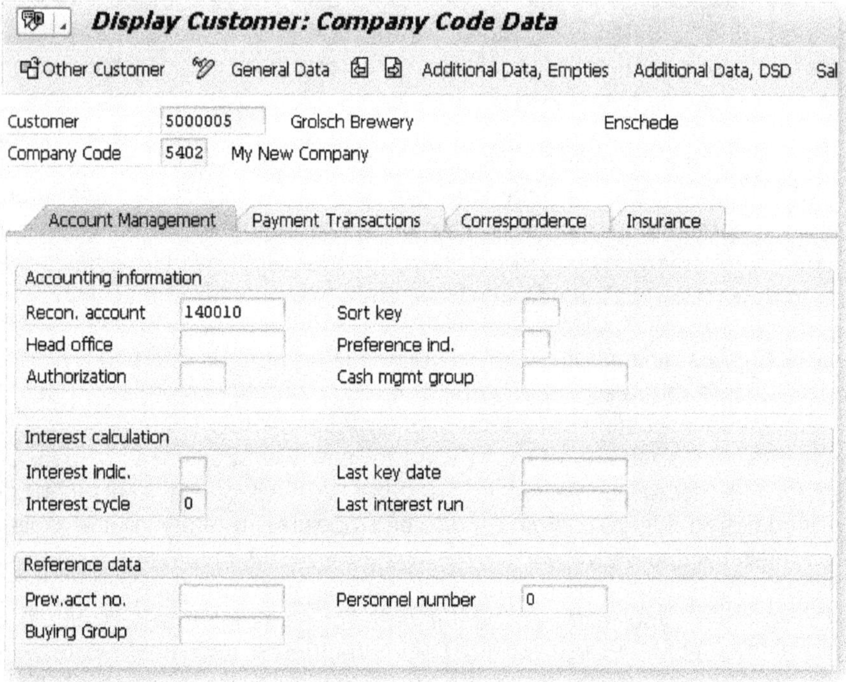

Figure 4.1: Customer master record

With the cursor placed on the field RECON. ACCOUNT, press the F1 key to display information about the field (Figure 4.2).

Click the TECHNICAL INFO icon to display information about the field and table, as well as the program and screen. (Figure 4.3).

Click ENTER CONTINUE or CANCEL to return to the customer display.

Figure 4.2: F1 (Help) for an SAP field

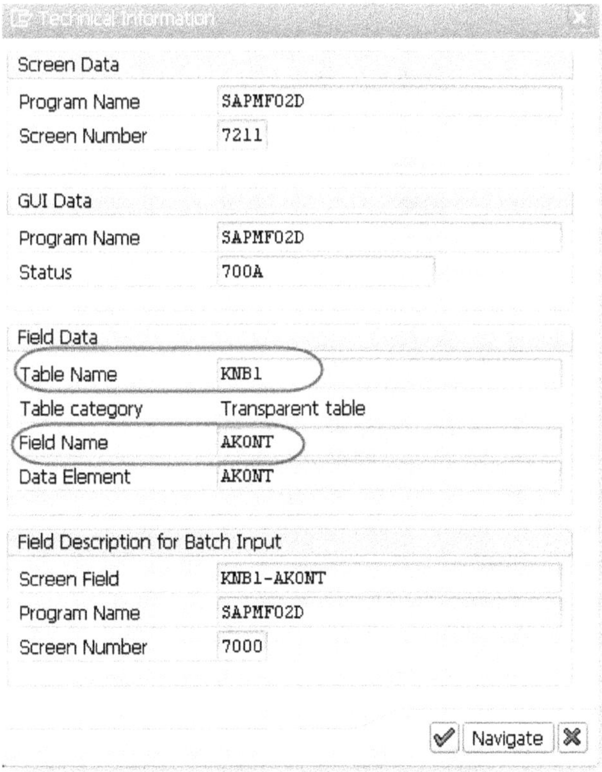

Figure 4.3: Display technical information for a field

4.1.2 Common SAP tables

The list of tables in the SAP system is quite extensive. The table below lists the most common tables related to SAP FI, AR, and AP.

Table	Description
T001	Company codes
KNA1	General data in customer master
KNB1	Customer master (company code)
LFA1	Vendor master (general section)
LFB1	Vendor master (company code)
BNKA	Bank master record
SKA1	GL account master (chart of accounts)
SKB1	GL account master (company code)
BSID	Customer accounting documents
BSAD	Customer accounting documents (cleared)
BSIK	Vendor accounting documents
BSAK	Vendor accounting documents (cleared)
BSIS	GL accounting document
BSAS	GL accounting document (cleared)
BKPF	Accounting document header
BSEG	Accounting document segment

4.2 Using SE11 to display table structure

SAP FI provides a transaction for creating, changing, and displaying database tables. It is likely that very few individuals in an organization will have access to create or modify tables. In fact, SAP-delivered tables should never be modified. However, there may be times when you need to understand a table structure.

To access the data dictionary function, navigate from the SAP EASY AC-CESS menu TOOLS • ABAP WORKBENCH • DEVELOPMENT • SE11 – ABAP DICTIONARY (Figure 4.4).

As mentioned above, you will likely only be allowed to display tables; enter the database table ID and click the DISPLAY icon &° (Figure 4.5).

Figure 4.4: Access SAP data dictionary

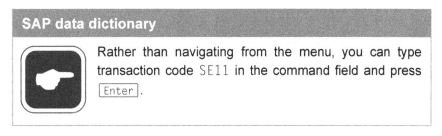

Figure 4.5: ABAP data dictionary, initial screen

The data dictionary for SKA1 is displayed as shown in Figure 4.6. The FIELDS tab is where you will find information about the fields in the table such as type (character, numeric, date), and length. Click the BACK icon ⊙ to return to the initial screen.

Dictionary: Display Table

⬅ ➡   🖫 ⬚   ⬚   ⬚   ⬚ 🖳 ☐ 🗆 ⬚ 🖽   Technical Settings   Indexes...   Append Structure...

Transparent Table	SKA1	Active
Short Description	G/L Account Master (Chart of Accounts)	

| Attributes | Delivery and Maintenance | Fields | Entry help/check | Currency/Quantity Fields |

    ☒ ☐ ☐ ☐   ☐ ☐ ☐ ☐   🔍 Srch Help   Predefined Type   1 / 19

Field	Key	Ini...	Data element	Data Type	Length	Deci...	Short Description
MANDT	☑	☑	MANDT	CLNT	3	0	Client
KTOPL	☑	☑	KTOPL	CHAR	4	0	Chart of Accounts
SAKNR	☑	☑	SAKNR	CHAR	10	0	G/L Account Number
XBILK	☐	☐	XBILK	CHAR	1	0	Indicator: Account is a balance sheet account?
SAKAN	☐	☐	SAKAN	CHAR	10	0	G/L account number, significant length
.INCLUDE	☐	☐	SI_SKA1	STRU	0	0	G/L Account Master Record (Chart of Accounts)
BILKT	☐	☐	BILKT	CHAR	10	0	Group Account Number
ERDAT	☐	☐	ERDAT_RF	DATS	8	0	Date on which the Record Was Created
ERNAM	☐	☐	ERNAM_RF	CHAR	12	0	Name of Person who Created the Object
GVTYP	☐	☐	GVTYP	CHAR	2	0	P&L statement account type
KTOKS	☐	☐	KTOKS	CHAR	4	0	G/L Account Group
MUSTR	☐	☐	MUSTR	CHAR	10	0	Number of the sample account
VBUND	☐	☐	RASSC	CHAR	6	0	Company ID of trading partner
XLOEV	☐	☐	XLOEV	CHAR	1	0	Indicator: Account marked for deletion?
XSPEA	☐	☐	XSPEA	CHAR	1	0	Indicator: account is blocked for creation ?
XSPEB	☐	☐	XSPEB	CHAR	1	0	Indicator: Is Account Blocked for Posting?
XSPEP	☐	☐	XSPEP	CHAR	1	0	Indicator: account blocked for planning ?
MCOD1	☐	☐	MCODF	CHAR	25	0	Search Term for Using Matchcode
FUNC_AREA	☐	☐	FKBER	CHAR	16	0	Functional Area

Figure 4.6: SAP data dictionary

Another handy function of the data dictionary is to find out where a table or field within a table is used. SAP FI provides a WHERE USED icon ⬚ for that purpose. The choices for where used are extensive and beyond the scope of this text; however, Figure 4.7, displays the programs that use the SKA1 table.

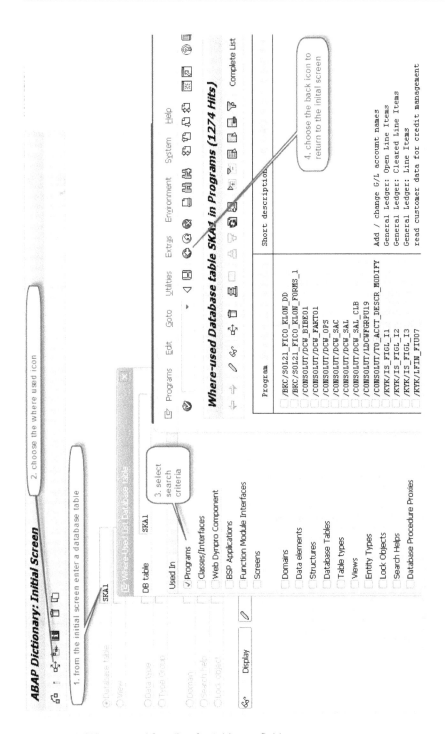

Figure 4.7: Where used function for tables or fields

127

4.3   Using SE16N to view table contents

Navigate to transaction SE16 to look at the actual data contained in a table.

From the SAP EASY ACCESS menu, go to TOOLS • ABAP WORKBENCH • OVERVIEW • SE16 – DATA BROWSER (Figure 4.8Figure 4.8).

However, transaction SE16N is a much more user friendly transaction to work with.

Figure 4.8: SE16 – Data browser

Rather than navigating to SE16, type SE16N in the command field and click ENTER 🗸 (Figure 4.9).

Figure 4.9: Access SE16N

For example, take a look at the records in table BSIS, which contains GL accounting transaction records. In the TABLE name field, enter BSIS. We want to look at only those records in the table for company code 5402, so enter 5402 in the COMPANY CODE FR. VALUE field and then click NUMBER OF ENTRIES. Figure 4.10 shows there are 36 accounting records in the table for company code 5402.

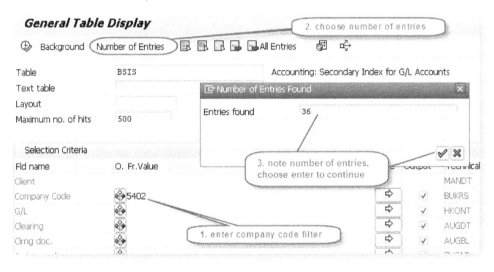

Figure 4.10: SE16N, count number of records

Now look at the actual records. You will note that there are many fields available for filtering and display. To filter on specific records, enter values in the FR. VALUE and TO VALUE fields. To choose to display only certain fields, selections are made in the OUTPUT column. The default is to display all fields. In   Figure 4.12, we only want to select a handful of fields, so we have deselected most fields and are only choosing the fields desired.

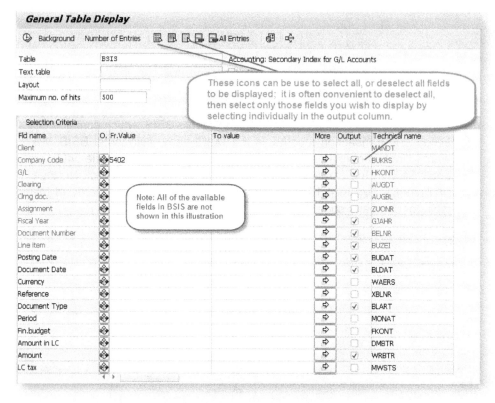

Figure 4.11: Figure 4.12: SE16N, filtering and field selection

With selections chosen, click the EXECUTE icon ⊕ to display the records (Figure 4.13). Note that only the fields chosen are displaying.

Exporting table records to an external application such as Microsoft Excel can be quite handy. Click the EXPORT icon 🖺 and follow the prompts to save the file on your local computer (Figure 4.13).

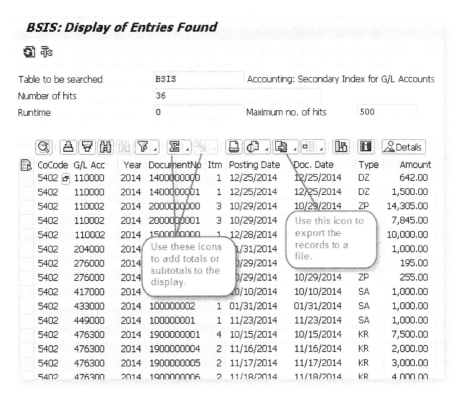

Figure 4.13: SE16 table records displayed

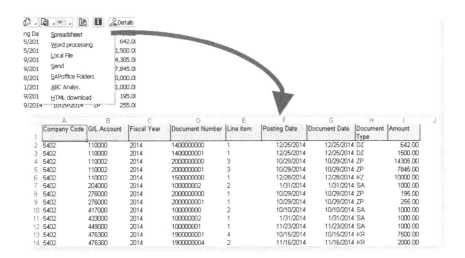

Figure 4.14: Exporting table records to Microsoft Excel

4.4 Using SQVI to view more than one table

There may be occasions when you want to combine fields from more than one table in your view. SAP FI provides a QuickViewer tool for just this purpose.

The steps below show how to create a simple query that combines fields from SAP tables KNA1 (general customer master data) with KNB1 (company code master data).

1. Navigate to TOOLS • ABAP WORKBENCH • UTILITIES • SQVI – QUICK-VIEWER (Figure 4.15).

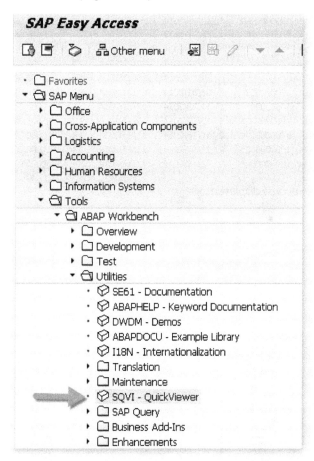

Figure 4.15: Create and execute QuickViewer Query, step 1

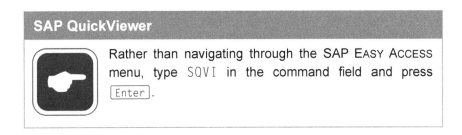

2. Enter a name for the query and click ⬜ Create (Figure 4.16).

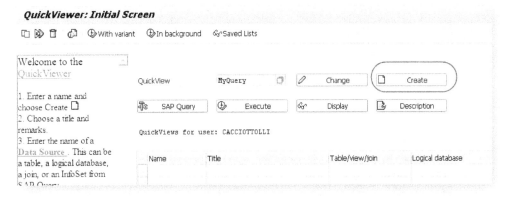

Figure 4.16: Create and execute QuickViewer Query, step 2

3. Enter a title for the query and select "Table join" as a DATA SOURCE from the dropdown menu (Figure 4.17). Then click ✔.

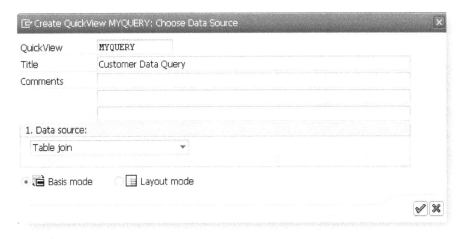

Figure 4.17: Create and execute QuickViewer Query, step 3

133

4. Click the INSERT TABLE icon 🔳, enter TABLE code "KNA1" and click the ENTER icon ✅. Repeat for table "KNB1" (Figure 4.18).

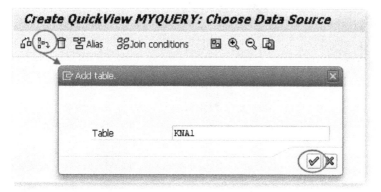

Figure 4.18: Create and execute QuickViewer Query, step 4

5. In Figure 4.19, you will note that SAP FI proposes table joins. If required, additional joins can be created by selecting a field from one table and dragging to select the field it should be joined to in the other table. In Figure 4.19, only the join proposed by SAP FI is used. Click the BACK icon 🔙 to continue creating the query.

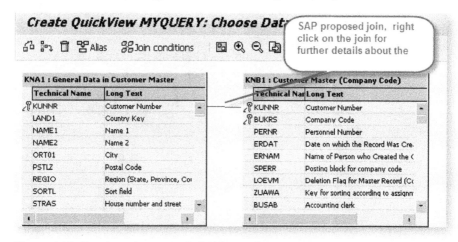

Figure 4.19: Create and execute QuickViewer Query, step 5

6. In Figure 4.20, we use the panel on the left to choose which fields from the tables to display and which fields to use for filtering the data. In the example, select the Name1 field to display from table KNA1. For table KNB1, mark CUSTOMER NUMBER and COMPANY CODE for display and selection, and PAYMENT TERMS just for display. Note that

as selections are made, the query design is displayed in the tabs on the right. Click the SAVE icon 💾 to save the query. Then click the EX-ECUTE icon 👇 to execute the query.

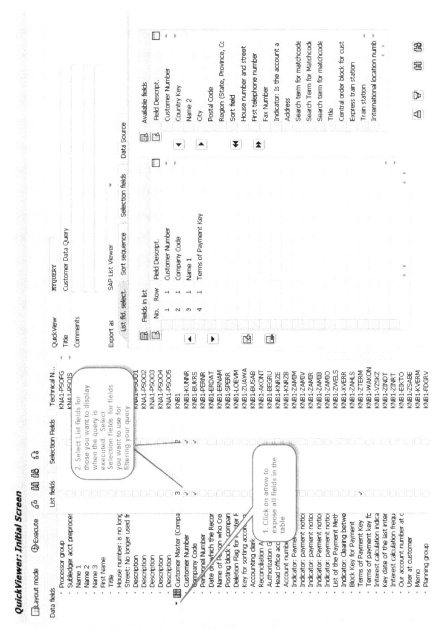

Figure 4.20 Create and execute QuickViewer Query, step 6

7. Next is a prompt for CUSTOMER NUMBER and COMPANY CODE since these fields were marked for selection when the query was created (Figure 4.21). Click the EXECUTE icon (⊕) to execute the query.

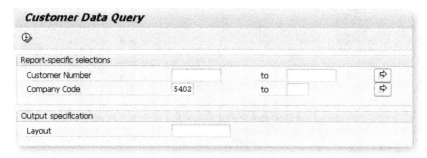

Figure 4.21: Create and execute QuickViewer Query, step 7

8. The query returns a list displaying records with selected fields (Figure 4.22). Click the BACK icon ⊗ once to return to the query criteria screen, twice to return to the query design screen, or three times to return to the SAP EASY ACCESS menu.

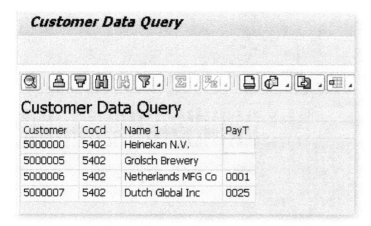

Figure 4.22: Create and execute QuickViewer Query, step 8

**espresso
tutorials**

You have finished the book.

A The Author

Ann Cacciottoli is a Specialist Senior with Deloitte, the world's largest private professional services firm. She has over 14 years of experience delivering SAP solutions, with a focus on SAP Financials and Reporting. She currently resides in Godfrey, IL. Her client-service work has taken her to Europe, Asia, and throughout the United States.

Ann has always been very passionate about sharing her knowledge and experience with those new to SAP.

B Index

C Disclaimer

This publication contains references to the products of SAP SE.

SAP, R/3, SAP NetWeaver, Duet, PartnerEdge, ByDesign, SAP BusinessObjects Explorer, StreamWork, and other SAP products and services mentioned herein as well as their respective logos are trademarks or registered trademarks of SAP SE in Germany and other countries.

Business Objects and the Business Objects logo, BusinessObjects, Crystal Reports, Crystal Decisions, Web Intelligence, Xcelsius, and other Business Objects products and services mentioned herein as well as their respective logos are trademarks or registered trademarks of Business Objects Software Ltd. Business Objects is an SAP company.

Sybase and Adaptive Server, iAnywhere, Sybase 365, SQL Anywhere, and other Sybase products and services mentioned herein as well as their respective logos are trademarks or registered trademarks of Sybase, Inc. Sybase is an SAP company.

SAP SE is neither the author nor the publisher of this publication and is not responsible for its content. SAP Group shall not be liable for errors or omissions with respect to the materials. The only warranties for SAP Group products and services are those that are set forth in the express warranty statements accompanying such products and services, if any. Nothing herein should be construed as constituting an additional warranty.

More Espresso Tutorials Books

Dieter Schlagenhauf & Jörg Siebert:

SAP® Fixed Assets Accounting (FI-AA)

▶ Processes and Functions in SAP ERP Financials

▶ Validation and Reporting for IFRS

▶ Posting Examples

▶ Periodic Activities Explained

http://5023.espresso-tutorials.com

Thomas Michael:

Reporting for SAP® Asset Accounting

▶ Basic asset accounting reporting features

▶ Balance, transaction and specialtity reports

▶ Asset history sheet and US tax reporting

http://5029.espresso-tutorials.com

Lennart B. Ullmann & Claus Wild:

Electronic Bank Statement and Lockbox in SAP® ERP

▶ Processing the Electronic Bank Statement in SAP

▶ Integrating Payment Advices as of SAP EhP 5

▶ New Functionality for Post-Processing as of SAP EhP 6

▶ Detailed Message Monitoring and Reprocessing Examples

http:/5056.espresso-tutorials.com

Stephen Birchall:

Invoice Verification for SAP®

- ▶ Learn everything you need for invoice verification and its role in FI and MM
- ▶ Keep user input to a minimum and automate the process
- ▶ Discover best practices to configure and maximize the use of this function

http://5073.espresso-tutorials.com

Janet Salmon & Ulrich Schlüter:

SAP® HANA for ERP Financials, 2nd edition

- ▶ Basic principles of SAP HANA
- ▶ The idea behind SAP Accounting powered by SAP HANA
- ▶ HANA applications in ERP Financials
- ▶ Implications on business processes

http://5092.espresso-tutorials.com

Ann Cacciottolli:

First Steps in SAP® Financial Accounting (FI)

- ▶ Overview of key SAP Financials functionality and SAP ERP integration
- ▶ Step-by-step guide to entering transactions
- ▶ SAP Financials reporting capabilities
- ▶ Hands-on instruction based on examples and screenshots

http://5095.espresso-tutorials.com

www.ingramcontent.com/pod-product-compliance
Lightning Source LLC
Chambersburg PA
CBHW071212050326
40689CB00011B/2304